Susan Seddon Boulet

The Goddess Paintings

TEXT BY Michael Babcock

With love and respect on your birthday & everyday. Tanya

POMEGRANATE ARTBOOKS • SAN FRANCISCO

Published by
Pomegranate Artbooks, Box 6099,
Rohnert Park, California 94927

Susan Seddon Boulet's paintings reproduced in this
book were rendered in oil pastel, ink and pencil.

Hardcover ISBN 1-56640-975-6
Paperback ISBN 1-56640-957-8

Library of Congress Catalog Card Number 93-87362

FIRST EDITION

Designed by Bonnie Smetts Design

Printed in Korea

Contents

The World of Myth

Approaching the subject of mythology is full of pitfalls, for myth serves so many functions. The word *myth*, denoting a narrative or story, possibly comes from an older root meaning "to yearn for"; it may ultimately derive from an Indo-European word meaning "to think, to imagine." We have tended to treat myths as older, fictional tales about gods and goddesses, stories with no basis in reality. But how is it possible for a mere story to grab our attention so strongly? How can a story appear and reappear in roughly the same form throughout different times and places in history?

Our new appreciation of mythology stems largely from the work of Carl Gustav Jung, who, with his followers, helped us understand the workings of the mind. The human psyche is neither rational nor logical. Its world is similar to the world of dreams: preverbal, nonlinear, present tense, nondualistic, multilayered, multivocal, symbolic and polyphonic. It is a world of images that transform into other images in the blink of an eye, a symbolic world more comfortable with metaphor and poetry than with concrete facts, symbols serving as a bridge between the unconscious and conscious minds. In the inner world, emotions, feelings and states of mind become personified, represented as a person, goddess, god or archetype.

ARCHETYPES . . .

Archetypes are the building blocks of the psyche, the organs of the soul. They are metaphors more describable by images than by words, entities easier to experience than describe. Jung likened the form of the archetype to the axial system of a crystal, which preforms the crystal's structure even though it has no actual physical existence itself. Nonetheless, archetypes are dynamic, energetic, their representations more a snapshot than the living reality. Archetypes are channels through which psychic energy moves; they are different possibilities of existence. We experience archetypes as personifications, as goddesses, gods or figures such as the Great Mother, the Wise Old Woman (or Man), the Divine Child. These entities are powerful images with their own life and energy: they have a fascinating, numinous quality.

The archetypes are universal, existing at the level of what Jung called the collective unconscious—the symbols, energies and images that are available to all humankind, distinct from the personal unconscious, which is particular to an individual. This shared unconscious explains how the same story can appear at different times and in different cultures. Although the archetypes are universal, their expression is personal: they come into existence through personal experience. These personified forces are not human; they are impersonal, dynamic energy not able to be contained within an individual person. One can be "possessed" by an archetype, so identified with it that the archetype, rather than one's own conscious mind or will, dictates actions.

Mythology appeals because it contains archetypes; it is a true story about our inner world. Jung, writing at the end of his life, wrote that it is only through myth that we can express what we are to our inward vision. Myths are told in the language of the psyche: dramatic, emotional, fantastic, symbolic and metaphorical. A particular myth draws us because it contains symbols important to our inner world, figures that somehow resonate deep in our psyche.

. . . AND GODDESSES

Goddesses are archetypal images, actual entities existing at the level of the collective unconscious. We do not invent the goddesses; bypassing our rational faculties, they come to us of their own accord, often quite unbidden. Even if their form is changed or lessened, they remain available to us through our psyche. A goddess enchants because even with a life of her own she represents a process in our own psyche, symbolizes a pattern in our own life: the overlapping symbols demand our attention. Somehow the goddesses and gods of myth that compel our attention are archetypes particularly relevant to our own psyche or story.

Thus a goddess is a metaphor, a sacred figure of the inner world, an image and symbol that speak directly to our psyche, linking our conscious and unconscious minds. Jung believed that healing results from contemplating the symbols that arise from one's unconscious: the symbol brings together body, mind and soul through the use of creative imagination. We must honor the symbols that present themselves to us, for they are the way the unconscious completes itself, becomes whole. We need myths and stories of goddesses and gods, for they feed the soul.

There is the Jungian idea of two different sides of the psyche: the feminine side and the masculine side. These two sets of traits have to do with groupings of characteristics and modes of being rather than biological gender. Female and male persons both have feminine and masculine consciousness. Feminine consciousness involves relationship, being, nature, the unification of opposites and the unconscious, or diffuse, mind; masculine consciousness involves logic, doing, culture, splitting into two and the conscious, or focused, mind. Western civilization has been grossly overbalanced in favor of the masculine: feminine values have been seen as inferior and not allowed free expression.

Since symbols serve an important function in the human mind and goddesses and gods (archetypes) are the organs of the psyche, it is critical that we have strong representations of both goddesses and gods to nourish our internal world. Inasmuch as divinities represent potentialities and possibilities, we need to have a full pantheon of female and male forms to inspire and set our imagination working, to give our inner world the richness and balance it requires.

APPROACHING THE SACRED

In the ancient world, goddesses and gods were a bridge to the sacred. A myth inspired awe because it resulted from a personal encounter with sacred energy:

it came from a face-to-face meeting with a numinous divinity that seemed to come from without, carrying a muscular life and energy all its own. Myth was the attempt to describe an overwhelming experience that defied explanation; it was the necessary response to an epiphany (the appearance of a goddess or god), a story about the awe-inspiring, ecstatic divine.

We live in a materialistic culture that denigrates both the sacred and the inner. This idea of living goddesses and gods somehow disturbs us. How ironic it is that we are now discovering powerful myths originating in "primitive" times, when the sacred was real and the profane merely a reflection of the sacred. From this standpoint, everything in the world is sacred. These cultures believed in nurturing the soul, another unpopular notion in our modern world. Goddesses and gods were real, sacred forces to be reckoned with. The current revival of mythology and the goddesses has to do with reexperiencing the reality of these forces; the renewed encounter with these living archetypes is a reexperiencing of the sacred.

The Buddhists have the notion of an ultimate energy, a place where everything exists in unity as One Being, One Suchness. The *Tao Te Ching* states that the Tao gives birth to the One, the One gives birth to the two, the two give birth to the three and the three give birth to everything else. Everything is traceable back to one impersonal source. The goddesses and gods are manifestations or vehicles of different aspects of this great impersonal energy: both are needed to represent the realm of possibilities. Each form ultimately receives its energy from the same source; each individual goddess goes back to the one Great Goddess and ultimately to that divine energy that is neither male nor female. This one universal energy, available to all, explains why similar goddesses have appeared all over the world.

In Tibetan Buddhism each of the various divinities represents an aspect of the psyche; by contemplating these divine energies you contemplate and activate them in yourself. The differentiation of goddesses into different types becomes a necessity, for it is difficult to relate to undifferentiated universal energy: we need to identify with an aspect, something concrete that can be contained in our minds.

THE SOCIOLOGICAL FUNCTION OF MYTH AND THE GODDESSES

According to Joseph Campbell, myth has four functions. The first is to impart a sense of awe about the mystery of being. The second has a cosmological dimension: myth explains the shape of the universe. In its third, or sociological, function myth supports and validates a certain social order. And fourth, myth has a teaching function: it shows us how to live and points the way to a spiritual life.

The sociological function of myth helps explain what happened to the goddesses. Myth, in addition to its other functions, always reflects a specific culture and social order. Nomadic hunters include in their mythology tales of the hunt, shamanic tales and vision quests. An agricultural culture focuses on myths that explain the growing cycle, the mystery of plants and foods. A patriarchal warrior culture produces myths with little softness, gentleness and nurturing. Myths reflect and validate a culture in a mutually reinforcing circle. The goddesses and gods of a society reflect its socially acceptable forms of divinity.

So why did the goddesses seemingly disappear? For the most part, over the past several thousand years only a few voices have spoken of the existence of powerful goddesses. Johann Jakob Bachofen wrote in the mid-nineteenth century of the existence of matriarchy prior to the historical era. Jane Ellen Harrison, writing at Cambridge in the early part of this century, discussed the goddesses who were a part of Greek mythology and also predated it. The English poet and novelist Robert Graves, writing in *The White Goddess* in 1948, wrote of the Great Goddess as the source of all poetry. The notes in his book *The Greek Myths*, first published in 1955, show the systematic transformation of powerful, all-encompassing goddesses into goddesses responsible for one small aspect of existence.

THE CIVILIZATION OF THE GREAT GODDESS

In the past few years we have been given compelling evidence for the existence of a time when the goddess reigned supreme. Marija Gimbutas has studied the archaeological evidence pertaining to the Neolithic period (roughly 6500 to 2500 B.C.) in the area she refers to as Old Europe, which encompassed western and eastern Europe down to the Mediterranean basin, including Greece, Turkey and the islands of the Aegean Sea.[1] She found evidence of a rich, sophisticated culture with all the components that define a civilization: conscious agricultural cultivation; animal husbandry; arts and crafts such as weaving, metallurgy, sculpture and pictorial arts; social organization; architecture; funerals; the beginning of script and writing. There were cities with 1,000 to 7,000 inhabitants in the sixth and seventh millennia B.C. Evidence shows continuous habitation of some areas for hundreds and even thousands of years.

This was a civilization of peace and beauty. Its structures and graves reveal a remarkable homogeneity in wealth and social status. This culture delighted in the natural world, constructed cities without walls in beautiful, undefended places, built magnificent tomb-shrines and temples and comfortable houses in moderately sized villages and created superb pottery and sculpture. Producing no weapons, it used metallurgy to create works of art. This was a long-lasting period of remarkable creativity and stability, an age free of strife with a culture focused on art.

The religion of the civilization was goddess based. Thousands of statues and figurines of goddesses have been uncovered from Neolithic Old Europe, hardly indicative of a mere cult barely worthy of consideration. Gimbutas depicts a coherent religion of consistency, clarity and great beauty. Yet, despite the thousands of statues and figures, historians have overlooked the civilization of Old Europe because they expected to find nothing. A peaceful, graceful, nonhierarchical culture does not fit our model of civilization as conquering, power-driven, hierarchical nation-states. If true religion must have a monotheistic god, there is no point in examining periods with a goddess-based religion.

The main motif of Old European ideology and art was the celebration of life. The main divinity, the most persistent feature of the archaeological record, was a parthenogenetic goddess, a supreme creator and the source of all life. Gimbutas explains the wide variety of figures as aspects of the one Great Goddess, whose core functions were life giving, death wielding, regeneration and renewal—a deity encompassing both the light and the dark. Symbols of regeneration and renewal always accompanied symbols of death; life was seen as continually transforming, just as the goddess transforms from one form to another. The symbols revolved around lunar rather than solar symbolism, the moon being a changing figure that waxes and wanes from darkness to light and back again to darkness. This Great Goddess was a complex, dynamic goddess concerned with all of life, upper and lower, with growth, decay and transformation. Not a mere fertility goddess, she was concerned with every aspect of existence; she gave the knowledge of arts and crafts as well as the life energy that begins and sustains all life.

It is completely natural that the first divinity be a woman. Awe of mystery and the thrill of confronting unknown, unexplainable things inspire religion. Feminine energy is naturally seen as transformative energy, for women somehow transform blood into life and give birth out of their own bodies. They produce milk to feed their infants. How could the original deity be anything but female?

So what happened to this culture of peace and beauty? Beginning in Europe in the middle of the fifth millennium B.C. there was a series of invasions by nomadic tribes who worshiped a sky god and a patriarchal mythology. A fierce, male-based culture seeking to extend its power and influence everywhere replaced the culture of the goddess. A righteous warrior god replaced the peaceful, transformative Great Goddess, and pastoral and patriarchal warrior gods replaced the prepatriarchal pantheon of goddesses and gods (there were a few). The new mythologies reflected and validated the new social and psychological orders.

Initially there was a superimposition of the patriarchal mythology, the masculine world of the Indo-Europeans, onto the goddesses of Old Europe. There was a process of fusion of symbols, some symbols from both worlds persisting side by side, others being transformed into new symbolic imagery and thus acquiring new meaning. In addition, many myths were consciously changed by the invaders to support the dominance of their gods.

Greek mythology reflects this addition, subtraction and combination of symbols and complexes of symbols. Some of the Greek myths (the abduction of Persephone by Hades; the rape of Hera by Zeus and their subsequent marriage) directly reflect the new order taking over the female agricultural mysteries of ancient times. Other myths (Apollo replacing Gaia and Themis as the oracle at Delphi) reveal male gods taking over functions once filled by goddesses. In Greek mythology goddesses were devalued and, in many instances, turned into mortals (for instance, Ariadne). The parthenogenetic supreme creators were minimalized or given one particular function. Thus Artemis became goddess of the hunt, Athena became goddess of wisdom and Hera became goddess of marriage. The nine muses, each responsible for a narrow area of creativity, were originally the triple-headed Great Goddess. Even so, traces of the older religion remained. In three different Greek versions of creation it is a goddess who is the original divinity and creator: Eurynome, goddess of all things; Gaia, the earth mother goddess; black-winged Night, feared even by Zeus.

The takeover of mythology was completed with Christianity and the Muslim religion. Here there are no female divinities but a parthenogenetic male god. Manifestations of goddess worship are seen as the work of the devil, which must be completely eradicated. Yet even here one finds traces: many followers of Christianity worshiped and still worship Mary, mother of Jesus, as divine, as a goddess. Thus in the sixteenth century Protestantism tried to banish Mary altogether.

REDISCOVERING THE GODDESSES

And yet goddesses are hard to banish. They retreated into the forests or the mountains and remained in various beliefs of the people, in folk tales and fairy stories. Now the cycle comes around, and the goddesses are beginning to reemerge.

Because the mind experiences different types of consciousness through archetypes, our options are limited when we lack adequate internal expressions of goddesses and gods, potentialities that inspire and present us with possibilities. It is no accident that with the arrival of patriarchy and the demise of goddesses, women were seen as inferior to men. Conversely, as women claim equal status and expanded possibilities for their lives, there is a burgeoning interest in goddesses.

We are now rediscovering and redescribing the goddesses of antiquity. Bereft of our own living sacred images, we return to existing goddesses. We cannot know exactly what the living reality of these goddesses was for the people who first discovered them; nonetheless, they have a timelessness that calls to us through the centuries and millennia. Despite all our sophistication, these goddesses and their symbols engage our attention. There is some way in which they nurture us at the very roots of our being.

Claude Lévi-Strauss founded the Structuralist interpretation of mythology, in which there is no one "true" version of a myth: each variation or experience of the myth belongs to the myth. In the same way, there is no one true version of a goddess. The figures of myth are continually being created and recreated. Thus the ancient mistress of wild animals and Greek goddess of the hunt, Artemis, and her Roman counterpart, Diana, can be seen as the same goddess, the same energy. As we discover these ancient images through symbol and story, our personal experience is part of a continuing myth.

We are partly rediscovering, partly reinventing the goddesses. We begin with whatever initial images present themselves to us: an ancient statue, a modern or ancient story, a symbol. As we learn about that goddess we personalize our experience of her, and her story is integrated into our own. As we read about the goddesses we find discrepancies or gaps: sources agree about some things and diverge widely on others. One book declares that Minerva was a preexisting Italian folk goddess and that the Greek figure of Athena was grafted onto her. One source states that Athena, the goddess of wisdom, was an original creator goddess. Another source relates her to the Old European parthenogenetic Bird Goddess, a birth and death goddess. Yet another relates that she was born out of the head of Zeus. Where do we find the reality of this goddess, this energy, this possibility?

Through reading, creative imagination and visual discovery we form images and feelings about a goddess, about her unique reality. The prehistoric forms of a goddess give us additional information, for there is great power still in these ancient images and figures. As we focus on the symbols congregating around her, we get a sense of qualities that are part of her makeup. For instance, the owl, an animal universally associated with death, is sacred to Athena; this indicates a relationship to death and transformation, even though no books talk about this aspect of her divinity. Ultimately we must judge by feeling. Jung describes feeling that is a means of making a judgment; he calls it a rational process (along with thinking). This is the feeling we must use. We must find what feels right, what fits our own inner reality, what is true to our own creative imagination. How does this figure resonate inside? We can allow the goddess herself to speak to us through our connection to the collective unconscious.

THE WORK OF SUSAN SEDDON BOULET

Often a goddess does not lend herself well to description in words, for she is a living, dynamic symbol. A goddess always contains aspects of many other goddesses. A visual image can speak directly to our unconscious, can show connections and arouse feelings. This is where the images of Susan Seddon Boulet come in. In many ways Susan, through her art, both recreates a goddess and creates her in a new form. A goddess is not merely a historical figure, something to be unearthed by archaeologists and displayed in a museum. Susan's work proves that the goddesses are very much alive today. She provides external, symbolic form to an inner reality, concretizing what we sense and feel into tangible, viewable form.

Something about Susan's work speaks directly to our psyches; some magic in them somehow claims our attention. She taps into that deep place in the psyche where images exist prior to words. Here is how Anaïs Nin described Susan's work in an introduction written in the 1970s and first published in *Shaman* in 1989:

> These figures are out of our dreams, those which flee from us upon awakening, those which are dispersed like dew at dawn, those which fall apart between our fingers like dust-roses.
>
> Susan Boulet has a more muted step, or perhaps she is invisible and more soft-voiced, soft-gestured, as the images do not escape from her. She can return from her voyages with intact descriptions...from places never visited by us but which we remember.
>
> Susan has her own mythology; it is of the elements which haunt our childhood and persist in our dreams....Her world is a rich, fecund one, an evanescent world usually eluding us, now in our possession.

Susan is known mainly through her book *Shaman*, published in 1989, magazines such as *Shaman's Drum* that have featured her work, and her yearly calendars. Although she has been "discovered" mostly in the past several years, she has a large, dynamic, evolving body of work that grows out of her life and roots.

Born and raised on a citrus and cattle farm in Brazil, Susan loved the freedom of the farm and its closeness to nature. Encouraged especially by her father, she began drawing as a child. Her first subjects were animals, the cows and horses of the farm, and there is movement and energy even in these first pieces. She has always enjoyed a rich fantasy life; as a young girl she loved the folk tales and fairy stories told by her father and caretakers on the farm. Later, while attending high school in Switzerland, she discovered the pageantry and history of the Middle Ages and the Renaissance.

After leaving school Susan lived and worked in Brazil until her marriage to Larry Boulet in 1967, when she moved to the San Francisco Bay Area. The birth of her son, Eric, in 1969 somehow helped to free her creativity. When she began selling her art, first at local crafts fairs starting in 1972, it was largely because of the encouragement of friends such as Marita Kallfelz and Kathy Davis. She credits Larry with providing much of the impetus to move outward; as she puts it, he did everything except paint: all of the organization, framing and detail work.

Most of Susan's formal training came in regular school classes, and a great deal of her artistic progress results from her own experimentation. Outside of school, she studied with people who conveyed their own great enthusiasm and love of art. From Monsieur Monet in Switzerland she learned the basics of oil painting. While in Switzerland she learned a great deal about color by observing the painted American magazine advertisements of the 1950s. Returning to Brazil after her schooling, she studied with an Italian sculptor in São Paulo, who taught her observation, attention to detail, sculpture and drawing. For a brief time she attended a commercial school of art in São Paulo. A friend, Donna Griffiths, introduced Susan to oil pastels, and her subsequent use of them came primarily through her own discovery and play. She still attends courses from time to time in such areas as figure drawing to continue her artistic development.

Susan's work shows a fascinating evolution over time. Her very early work is marked by simplicity and mystery. Other early work has a medieval flavor, with its wimpled figures with round faces dressed in the clothing of dreams. Much of her work from the 1970s (her son was born in 1969) contains themes from fairy tales: princesses and princes, dragons, children, unicorns, wood nymphs, spirits and fairies. The Aphrodite found on page 23, painted in October 1978, is representative of her work in the 1970s.

Susan's paintings are usually a combination of pastel, either oil or dry, pencil and ink. She began working with oil pastels soon after moving to the United

States in 1967 and added dry pastels in the late 1980s. Initially she worked on crescent board and used sharp tools to etch out details and create fine lines. She uses ink as a wash, a technique discovered early on by accident: when she spilled some ink on a piece she liked the resulting texture, so she began to develop it into her work.

Sometime around 1980, she switched from crescent board to four-ply rag (acid-free) paper. This new paper was thicker and less smooth, allowing her to experiment and play with textures and multiple layers in a new way. After starting to use this paper she resumed her interest in pencil and began to incorporate it into her work, especially to create detail. Soon after, she produced two images that pointed to the new direction she would take: her first real shamanic figure (*I Heard the Owl Call My Name*, from her book *Shaman*) and the *Isis and Osiris* included in this collection. Over time we see a greater mastery of her materials as the figures become more complex and multilayered, more integrated; forms flow more easily into and out of one another. More than half of the work in this book dates from 1988, from the maturing of her art.

Susan begins work with a seed idea, a form, symbol or request: a place to start. She begins carefully, wanting to produce a very "elegant, clean piece." Her real work begins after she simply dives in and destroys the whiteness of the page. She may begin by applying color, or she may apply the texture first. Texture, as we can see, is extremely important to Susan. She applies it in a number of ways: by layering oil or dry pastels, by drawing or by using colored ink. She is fascinated by detail, by the process of creating the texture of a feather as she draws, watching as an animal emerges from a shadow.

Susan's art is a joint process of discovery and invention. As much as possible she works without a final image in mind, because a piece often takes on a life of its own as the creative flow and inspiration lead her in unexpected directions; often her subjects simply "don't want to be corralled." At times she feels she has ruined a piece and scrapes off all the pastel, only to find another image already there.

> Sometimes, if I get tired I'll end up, perhaps, destroying something that might have been useful to keep. But then that leads me somewhere else too, and that creates another picture. So within a picture there are probably ten pictures, more often than not.

She works best when she works on four or five pieces at once; this is one way to keep a distance, to keep seeing a piece with new eyes. She uses her feeling sense and intuition to know whether something is working or not. As she paints or draws she finds herself in a very quiet place, a process akin to meditation: "It's observing but not holding onto any image. It's like being an observer in the flow of ideas, in the flow of image." She keeps working until "all of a sudden something internal says: 'That's it.' And it's finished....All of a sudden the pieces that are there work and then it's finished."

Susan's paintings have to do with storytelling: they are Susan telling stories to herself, watching the stories evolve. As in dreams, the symbols and figures of a painting emerge from Susan's psyche, echoing themes from her unconscious world that demand attention. An outward expression of her inner world, her work is thus a reflection of her own process, which she consciously uses as a tool for self-understanding and self-exploration. Thus she frequently returns to myths, such as that of Psyche and Eros, that have particular meaning for her; the portrayals she paints lend insight into her inner world. The paintings sometimes reflect what she is comfortable with: she might paint the loving Aphrodite blessing Eros and Psyche rather than the jealous goddess who gave Psyche impossible tasks to perform. In other instances she explores new ideas, symbols and modes of being through her art, approaching them in a mythic or symbolic way first in order to integrate them into her life later. It is sometimes the events in her life that push her in new directions, cause new deepenings. One of the biggest changes in her work came as a result of the death of her husband, in 1980. The Persephone on page 90 is an example of the work that has grown out of her experience with breast cancer, which forced her into a new exploration of her own ground.

Susan views her work as a continuum, an evolution. Her later images are more mature, reflections of her growth through life, her passage through time. What once would have been Merlin the Magician is now a Wise Old Man or a Native American elder; what once was a medieval maiden untouched by time has become a mature queen or a wise grandmother marked by her years. Her earlier representations of Eros and Psyche have to do with the earlier stages of the story, when Psyche was still unable to look upon Eros. Her later representations, such as those in this book, have more to do with the end of the myth, with the point at which Psyche had matured enough to integrate all the parts of herself and had become capable of truly loving—first herself, and then Eros. Susan feels that her work has become much more connected to her life: the figures in her later work are somehow more weighty, more powerful, deeper-level archetypes. There is a power and groundedness to many of her most recent images.

MYTH AND THE GODDESSES

Although Susan's paintings are her own self-expression, there is also a universality to them. She feels that her works come from the collective unconscious, from a place to which we all have access, understood at some deep, not necessarily intellectual, level. Because paintings are nonverbal, they cut through the confusion that language can sometimes cause. People often feel as if she has painted the image of a secret place found in their own inner world.

If Susan's work is mythic, it is because myth is something that happens eternally in the present. If she paints figures from "ancient" myth it is because they have relevance for her here and now:

> I think that myth is the story that comes to us from the beginning of time. So that, for me, it becomes ageless.... It really is no more ancient for me now than I'm sure it was at the time it was created. It's simply that maybe when we go into the mythic realm we go beyond time, or we go into time or where time doesn't exist—it's the timeless place from where I think myth comes because myth has relevance to our lives today as it did then.

Susan has always painted goddesses. She paints more goddesses than gods, more female than male figures, and the male figures themselves are often somewhat androgynous. The goddesses are easier for her, more familiar; there is a stronger inner connection. Susan sees the goddess paintings as a direct reflection of herself, an extension of her own inner world. They are, in her words, "containers for the development of an idea and ways of looking at my own feminine nature." They are ways of discovering different aspects of herself.

In fact, painting a goddess is not much different from painting anything else: she is simply telling a story. She chooses the figures she does because there is some appeal, interest or connection: the imagery must spark something inside. As always, she starts with an idea, symbol or image and follows it where it wants to go. There might be a story line she is interested in. Sometimes she sees something that grabs her attention, say a beautiful pair of wings, and begins by drawing in a figure that then becomes a goddess. These paintings are only as miraculous as her other work.

This book contains fifty-nine different paintings of goddesses, reflecting Susan's work mostly over the past several years. They are primarily images of western European goddesses, with a few from Native American and other world cultures. Reflections of Susan's psyche, they are also representations of subjects that demanded expression, images that were available to be discovered or invented by Susan. They are new renderings of ancient, still-living goddesses made available to our modern world. There are images that will speak directly to each of us in different ways. Some pieces will reveal something we knew and had not thought of in years, perhaps ever. We will see glimpses of ourselves that we have sensed before but have never been able to label or describe verbally. Other pictures will draw our attention and claim it, leaving us moved beyond words. Together, these pictures are a celebration both of Susan's work and of the possibilities for feminine existence, modes and potentialities that span the breadth of life.

NOTE

1. The following material about the flowering of Old Europe and its subsequent demise is based largely on the work of Marija Gimbutas in the following three books. Although some consider Gimbutas controversial, her books are an eloquent, exhaustive examination and statement of the archaeological evidence for Neolithic Old Europe.

Gimbutas, Marija. *The Goddesses and Gods of Old Europe*. Berkeley & Los Angeles: University of California Press, 1982.

Gimbutas, Marija. *The Language of the Goddess*. San Francisco: HarperCollins, 1989.

Gimbutas, Marija. *The Civilization of the Goddess*. San Francisco: HarperCollins, 1991.

Amphitrite

Amphitrite is the ancient sea goddess of the Greeks. The original Great Goddess in her aspect as ruler of the oceans and seas, she is responsible for all of the life of the sea. She lives in the far western ocean in a golden palace filled with precious gems, where she loves to spin and sing. She is often portrayed with long, flowing hair, a symbol of vitality, strength and creative energy. This goddess reflects the character of the ocean as primordial creation and inexhaustible vital energy, a place of hidden treasure and unending wealth. Amphitrite represents the ability to express the full range of emotions, from placid calm to raging storm, the ability to move through the depths of the collective unconscious.

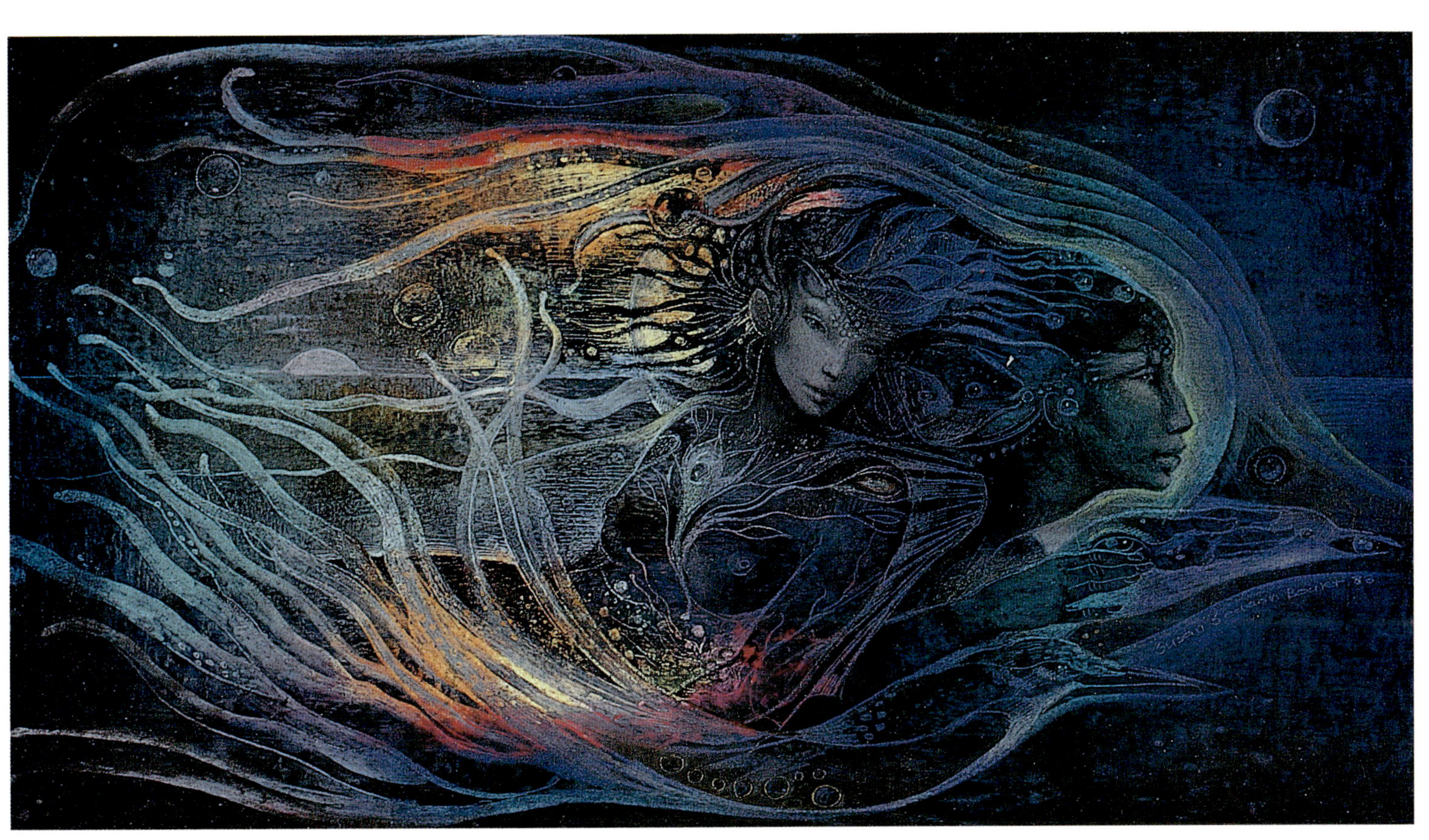

Aphrodite

Aphrodite is most often described as radiant and shining: when Aphrodite is present the whole world acquires a soft, golden glow. "Foam born," she is associated with the creative, life-giving sea and represents a sense of freshness, renewal and hope. A descendant of the prehistoric water bird goddesses of Old Europe, she is often accompanied by birds. The goddess of both spiritual and passionate love, Aphrodite joins us to one another. She is feminine being in all her fullness, and her realm is that of relationship and feeling. One of the paintings shows her in the form of a dove, embracing her son, Eros, and his wife, Psyche. This moment depicts the point at which Psyche, having completed the tasks assigned her by Aphrodite, is reunited with Eros—the point at which a new and renewed relationship with love is possible. This moment reveals an Aphrodite who demands maturity if we are to be in true relationship: when we embrace mature love, Aphrodite is there to bless us.

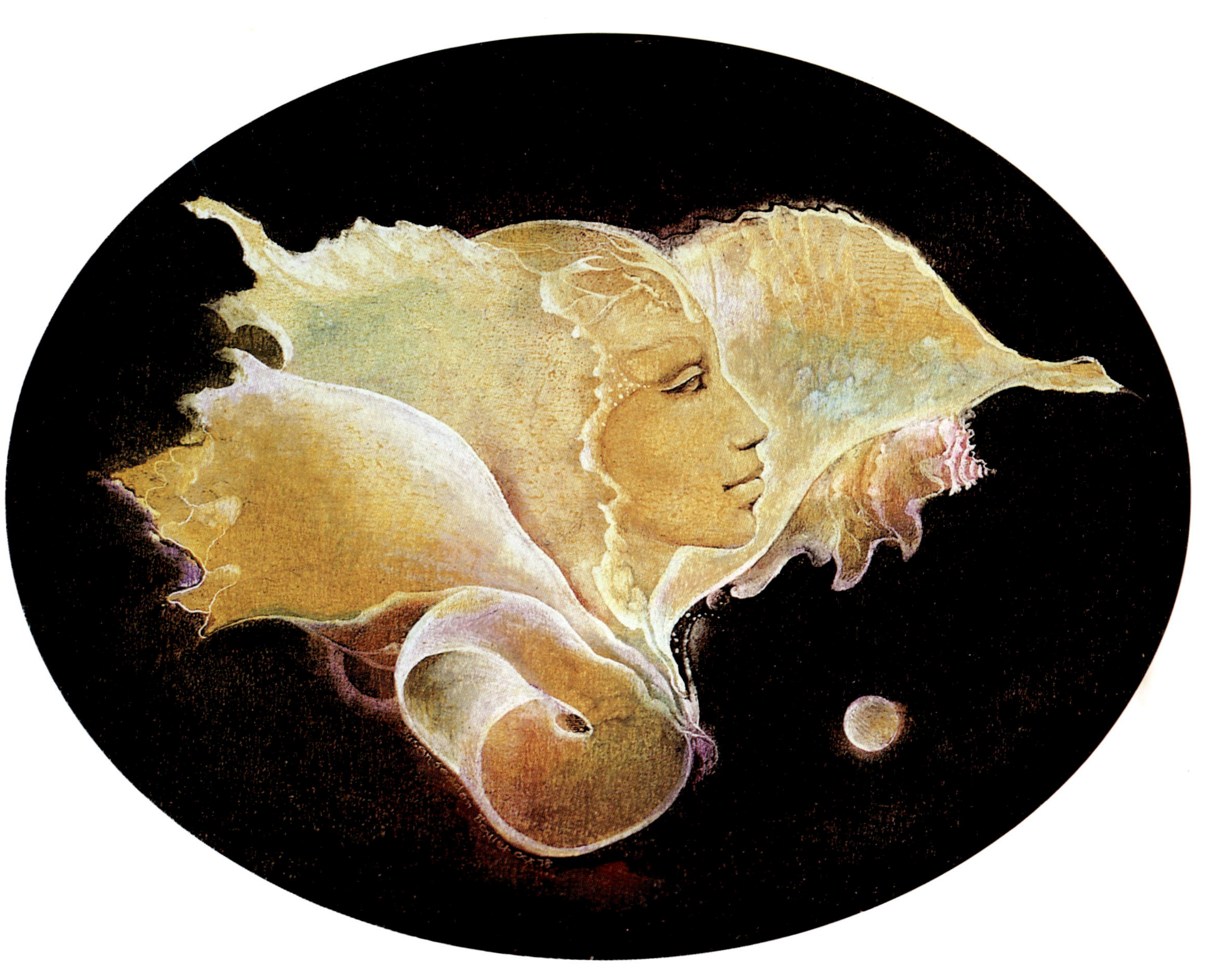

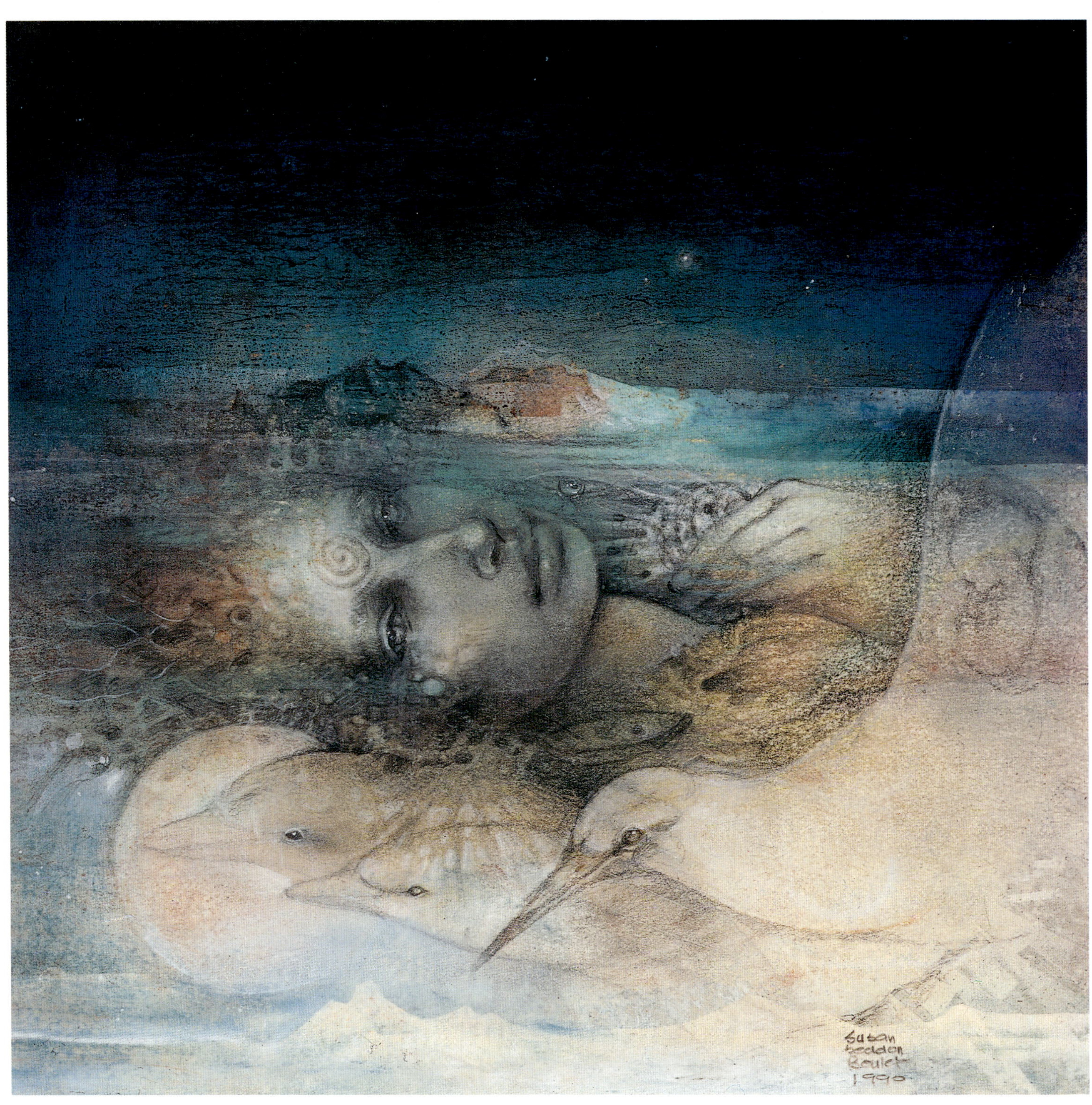
Susan
Seddon
Boulet
1990

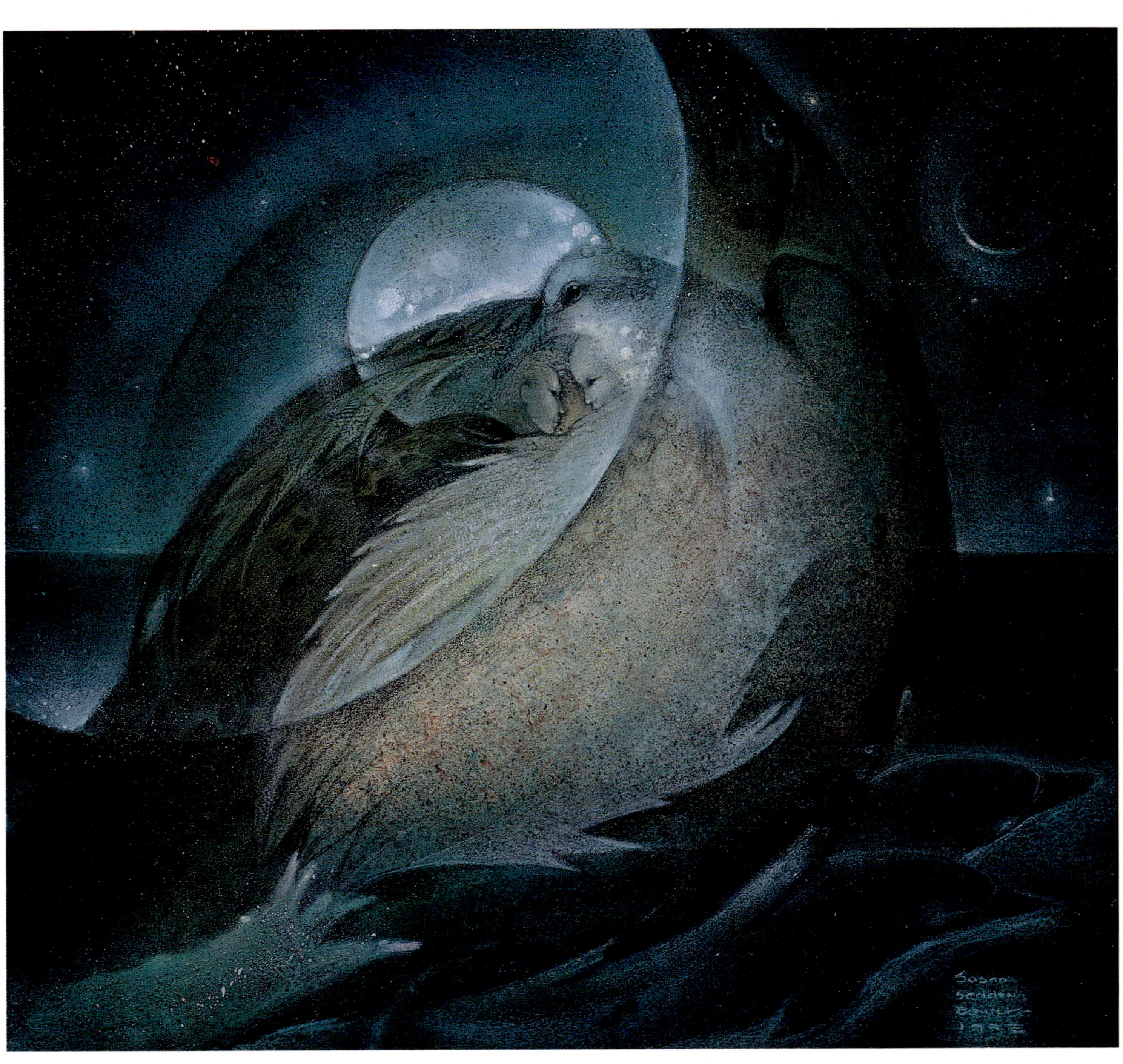

Artemis and Artemis Calliste

Artemis, the archaic mistress of animals, probably dates back to Paleolithic times. Her realm is the wilderness, and her concern extends to all wild, untamed things. She presides over the hunt and is the goddess of hunters. Fiercely individualistic and independent, she remains apart from relationship to men. Despite her fierceness she is addressed as a healing and soothing goddess. Protector of births, she alleviates the suffering of women in childbirth. She is also responsible for the initiation of young girls. As Artemis Calliste (Artemis, the Fairest) she takes on the form of the bear-mother, fiercely protective of her young, independent and completely in touch with her instinctual nature. Artemis is a wonderful symbol of female independence. She reminds us of the value of solitude and the importance of wild, unprotected places. She shows us those frightening places that bring healing even through fear.

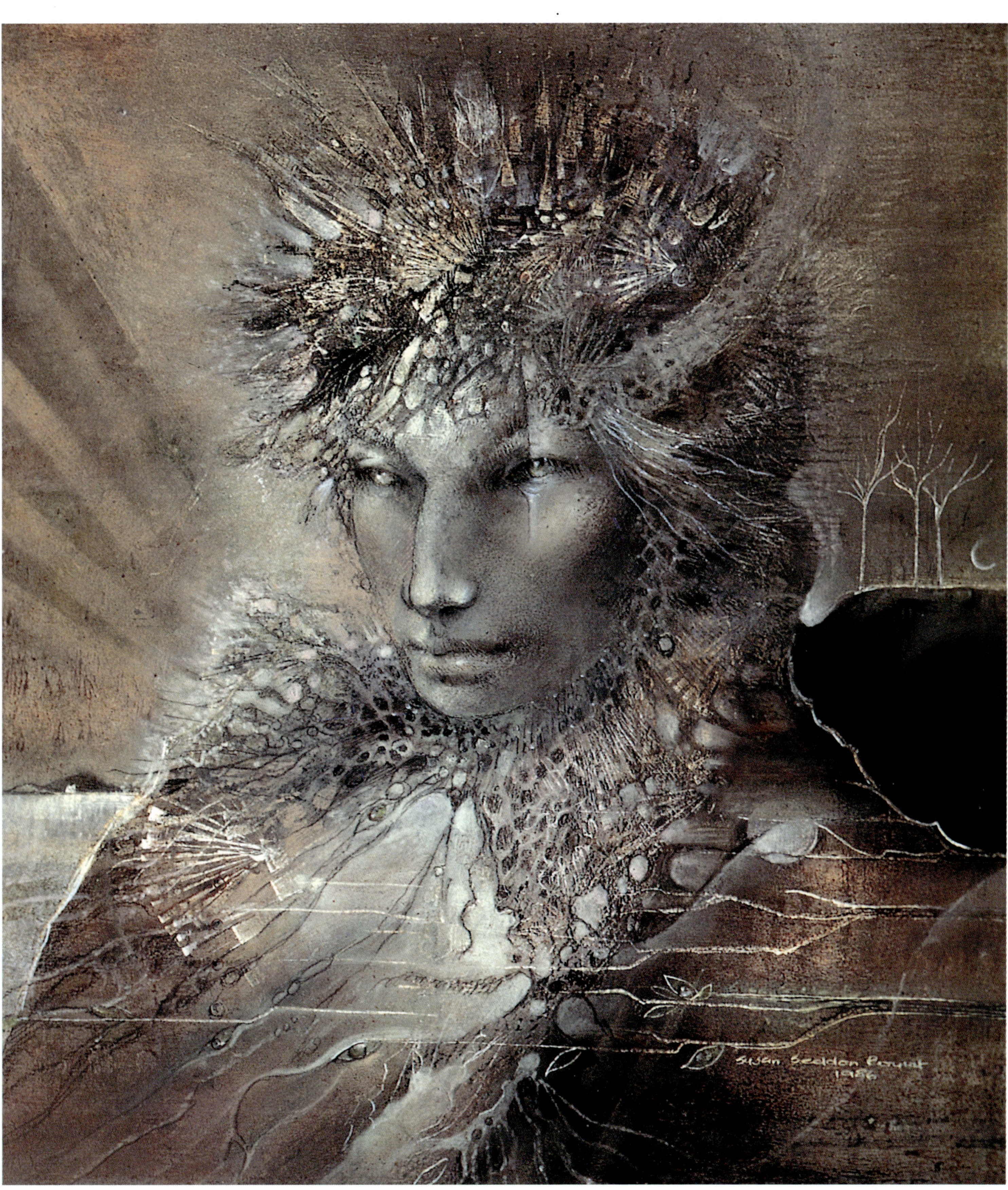
Susan Seddon Boulet
1986

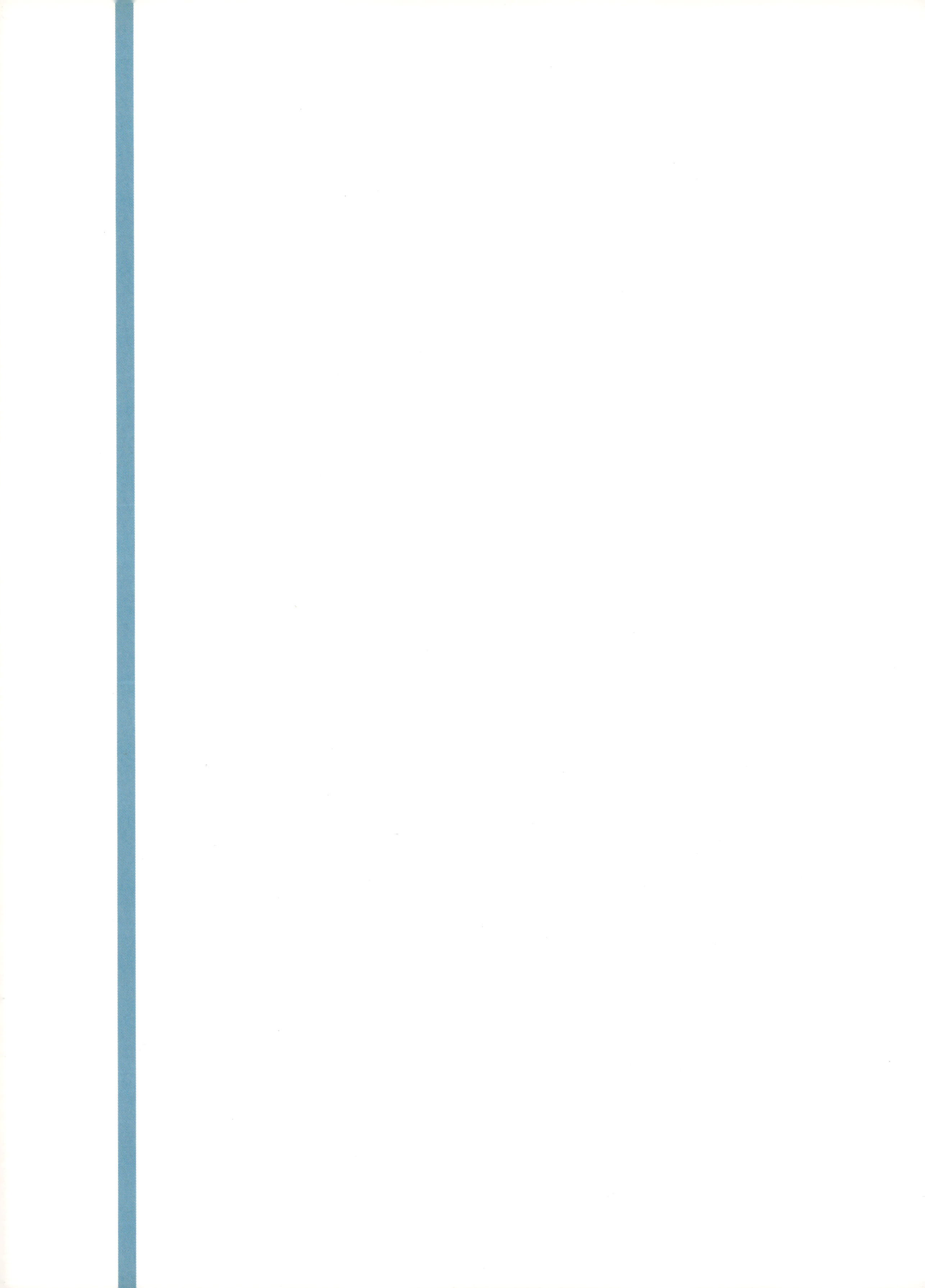

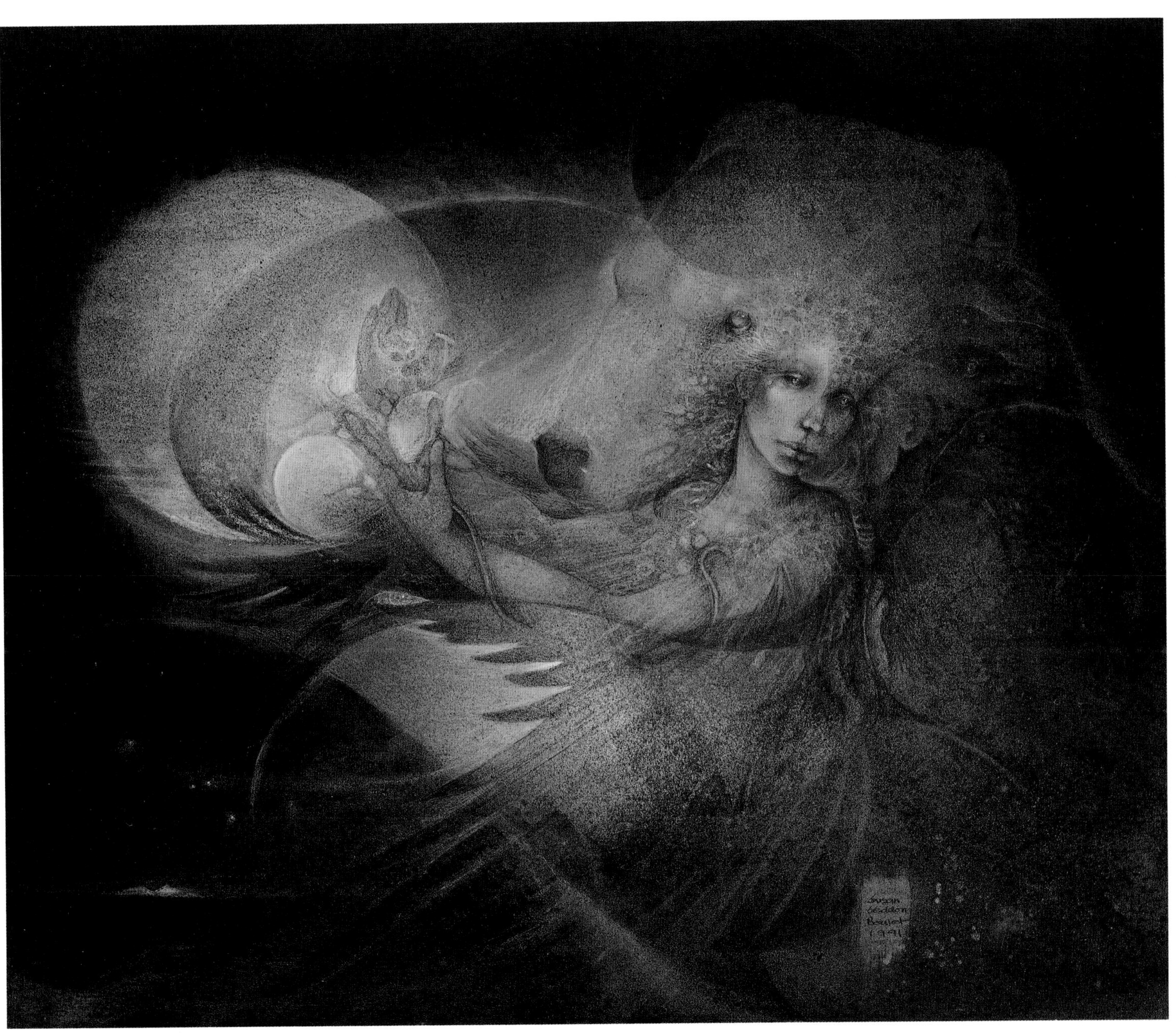

Astarte

Astarte is an ancient Phoenician Great Mother goddess. Also known as Astoreth or Ashtoreth, she is related to both Isis and Aphrodite. Astarte is the Queen of Heaven, the Guiding Star, the Sovereign of the World, the Splendid Lasting Light. As the morning star, Mars, she is the goddess of war, and as the evening star, Venus, she is the goddess of love and desire. Her horns are either the crescent moon, in her guise as the moon-goddess creator-preserver-destroyer, or the horns of a cow, representing fruitfulness, generation and productivity. She is especially connected with fertility and with the life-force of sexual energy and desire. Each winter she descends to the underworld to retrieve her lost lover. Astarte is a figure of pride in feminine being, a celebration of the abundance that comes from the energy of a woman in touch with herself and her body.

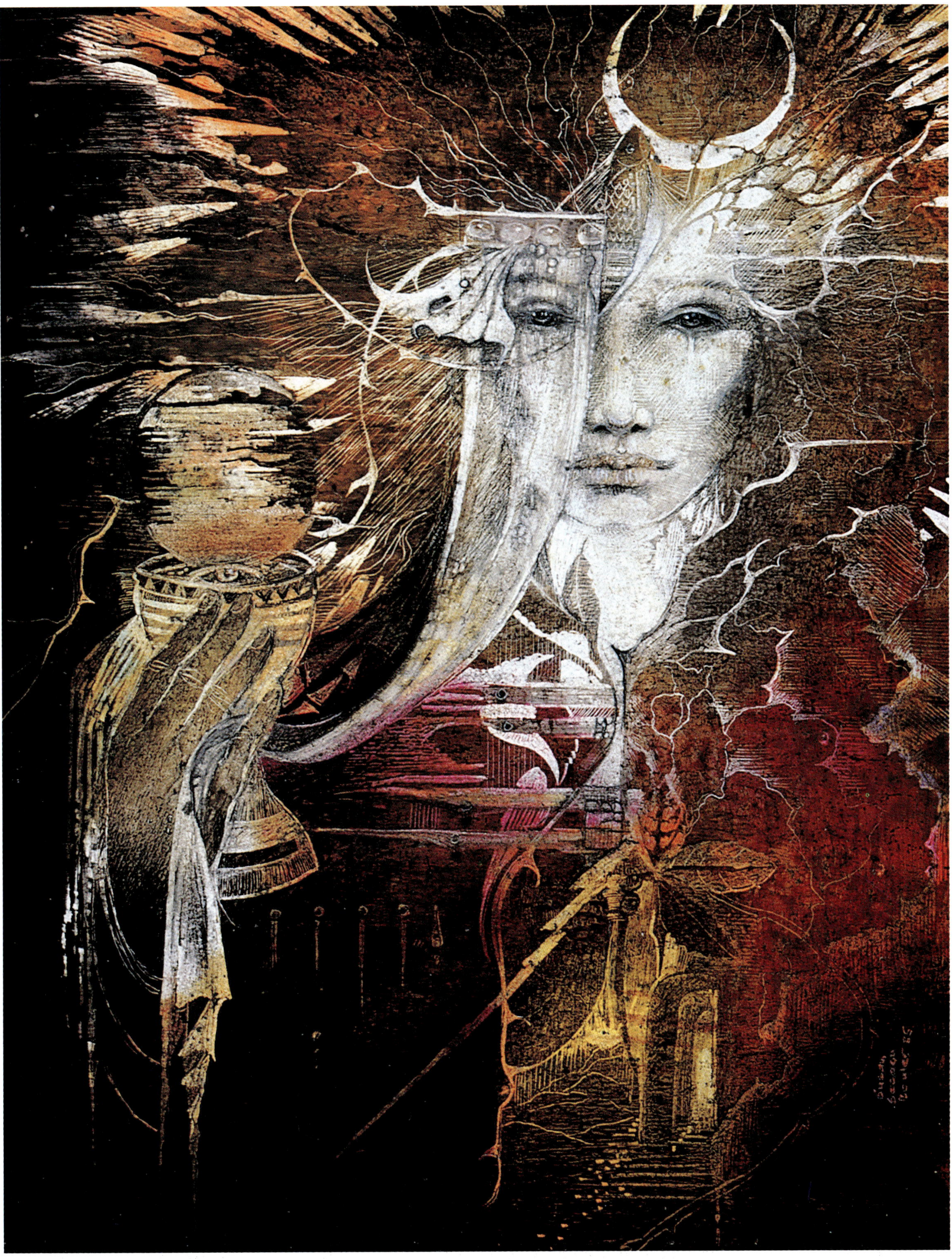

Athena

Athena is presented by the Greeks as the virgin goddess of war and wisdom. A symbol of courage and friendship, she often counsels warriors to gentleness. She is especially honored as a goddess of agriculture, the creator of the olive tree, the flute, the ship, goldsmithing and shoemaking and the goddess who introduced the yoke for the oxen and the bridle for the horse. She is a patron of all useful and elegant arts.

Athena's original guise was more inclusive and powerful. She was the prehistoric, parthenogenetic Bird Goddess, both creator and destroyer. One of her forms was that of a serpent, a universal symbol of life energy and life force. She invented all of the crafts used by men and women. In Greek mythology she is said to have breathed soul into the men created by Prometheus and to have helped Prometheus steal fire from the heavens to give to men—somewhat distorted forms of a goddess who did not need Prometheus to do these deeds. Athena is a wonderful affirmation that there are no limits to what a woman can do with her intellect and creative ability.

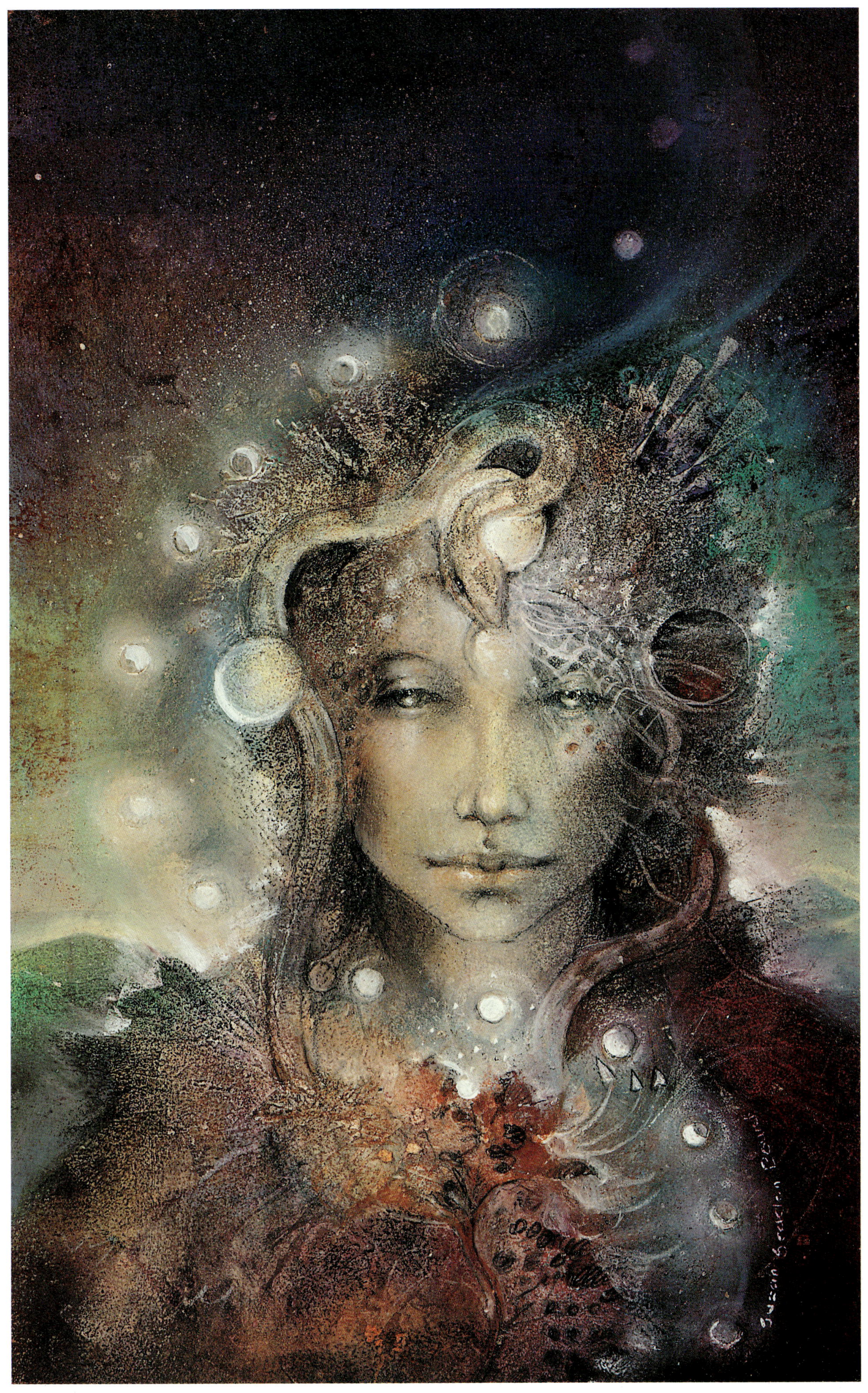

Bast

Bast (or Bastet, or Pasht) was the Egyptian goddess who appeared in cat form. The Egyptians highly revered cats; the word for cat, *mau*, also denoted light and was cognate with the word for mother. The cat is a lunar animal and also a solar animal representing the power of the sun as reflected in nature. Since the cat is an earth animal, Bast is also an earth mother goddess, a giver of life and abundance. In touch with her wild, instinctual nature, she also is a protector of women during childbirth. Like a cat, she is fiercely independent and belongs to no one but herself. Bast is one of the more joyful goddesses; her elaborate festivals in the town of Babustis were renowned for their joyful dancing.

Embodying a cat's gentler aspects, Bast is a personification of life and fruitfulness. The quintessential life-affirming mother, she reminds us to be playful and relaxed like a cat and to find occasions to celebrate life.

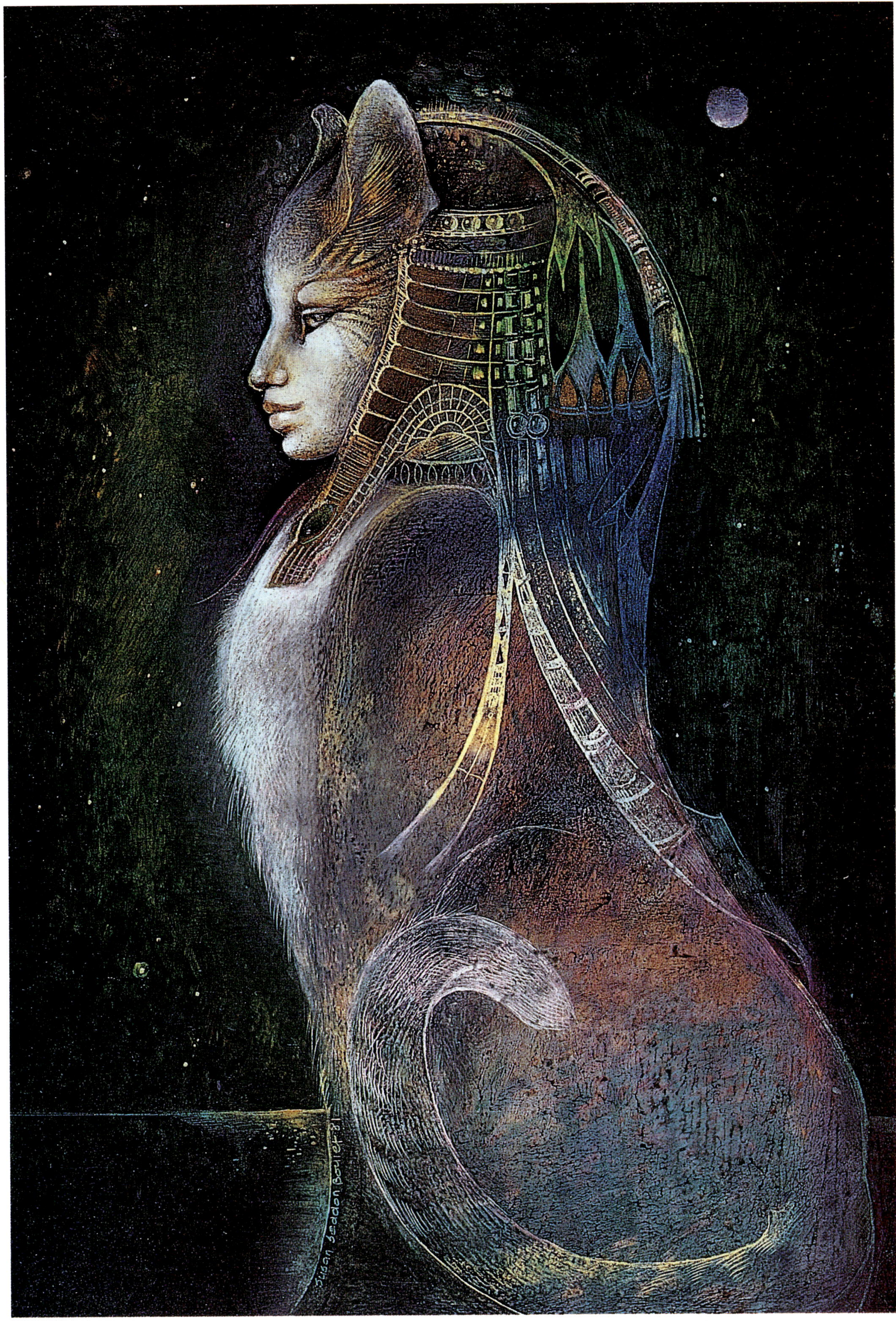

Bird Goddess

The Bird Goddess is one of the oldest representations of female divinity, dating back to Paleolithic times, nearly 15,000 years ago. The Bird Goddess rules over everything, both the land of the living and the land of the dead. She is the parthenogenetic life giver, creator of all life energy, health, abundance, nourishment and material goods. She is the Goddess of the Hunt, the Lady of the Waters, the Nourishing Mother. She is the goddess of death and taker of life as well as the regeneratrix and goddess of transformation, initiation and rebirth. The presence of this goddess was felt everywhere: on earth, in the seas, in the heavens and beyond. This goddess reminds us to acknowledge all the parts of ourselves, for there is no place that does not belong under her guidance. She is a reminder to be life givers connected to our instinctual, animal nature. She tells us that we too can soar to the heavens.

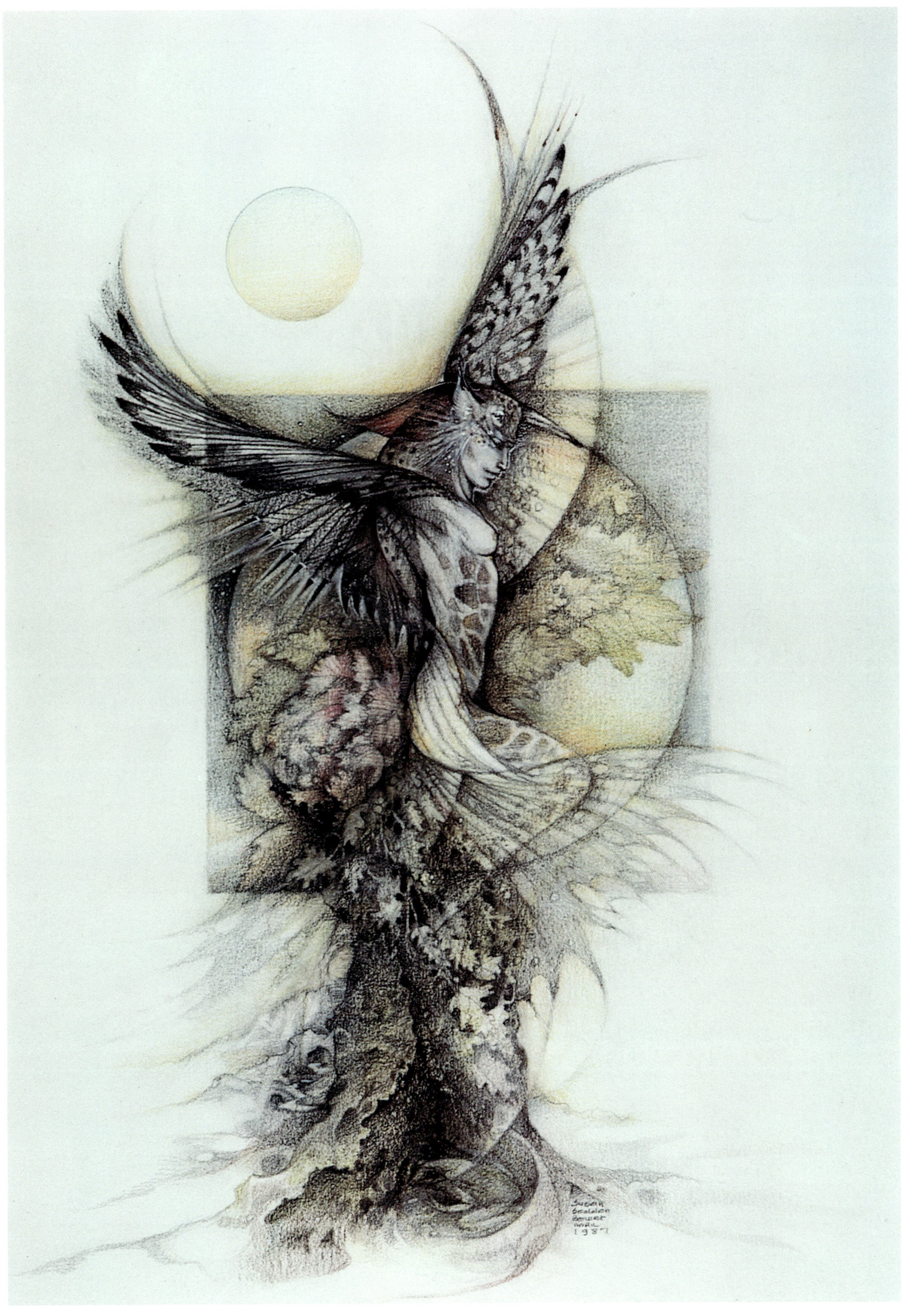
1987

Changing Woman

Changing Woman is perhaps the most revered of deities among the Native Americans of the southwestern United States. She is a wholly benevolent figure, for it is Changing Woman who gives the people their abundance and who provides the teachings that allow them to live in harmony with all things. In the initiation ceremony of Navajo women, the initiate takes in the power of Changing Woman so that she might learn the values of love, hospitality and generosity and know that she herself is a source of food and harmony. Also called Earth Mother, Changing Woman is said to be identical with Mother Earth, the earth and all of nature being her outer form.

Changing Woman received her name because she can change at will from a baby to a girl to a young woman to an old woman and then back again. Very much alive today, she is a tremendously nourishing goddess who teaches the cycles of birth and death and the wisdom of nature.

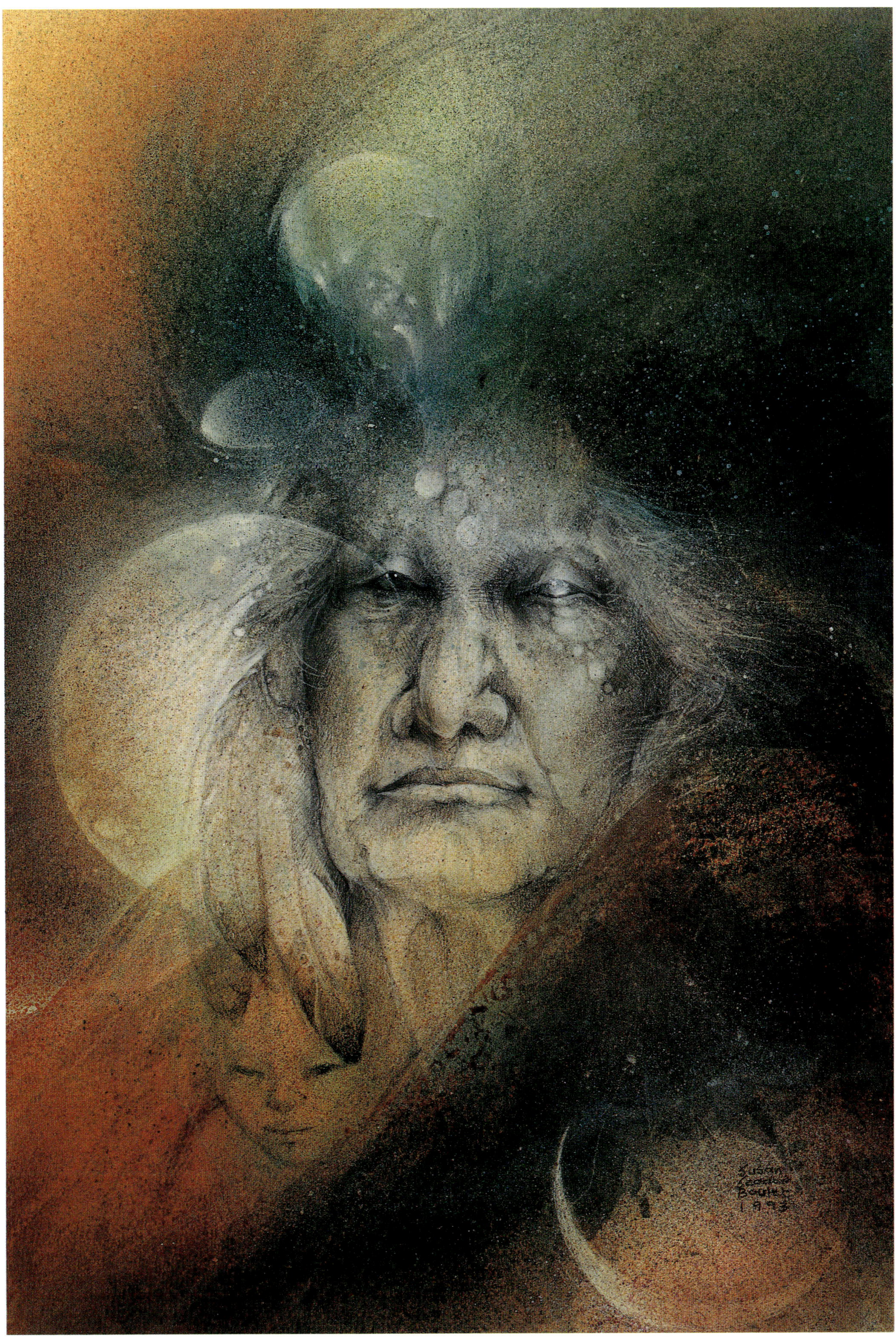

Diana

Diana is the ancient Lady of the Beasts, called by the Romans Lucina, Goddess of the Light. As mistress of wild things she is especially responsible for anything young and vulnerable, be it wild or human. She is a goddess of solitude, comfortable with the wilderness and with the great silences of nature. She represents the mystic, primitive identity of the hunter and the hunted.

Diana is a moon goddess, symbolizing the moon in its crescent phase, shown by the diadem she wears. She stands for the virgin, a self-sufficient, free goddess who lives life on her own terms. Especially a goddess of women, she is related to all phases of female existence, from infancy to menstruation through birth, nursing, menopause and death. Diana is another goddess ancient women called upon for protection and help during childbirth. Diana stands for the part of us that is at home in the wildness, at home with our primitive, instinctual nature. She is the midwife and protector of the Divine Child within.

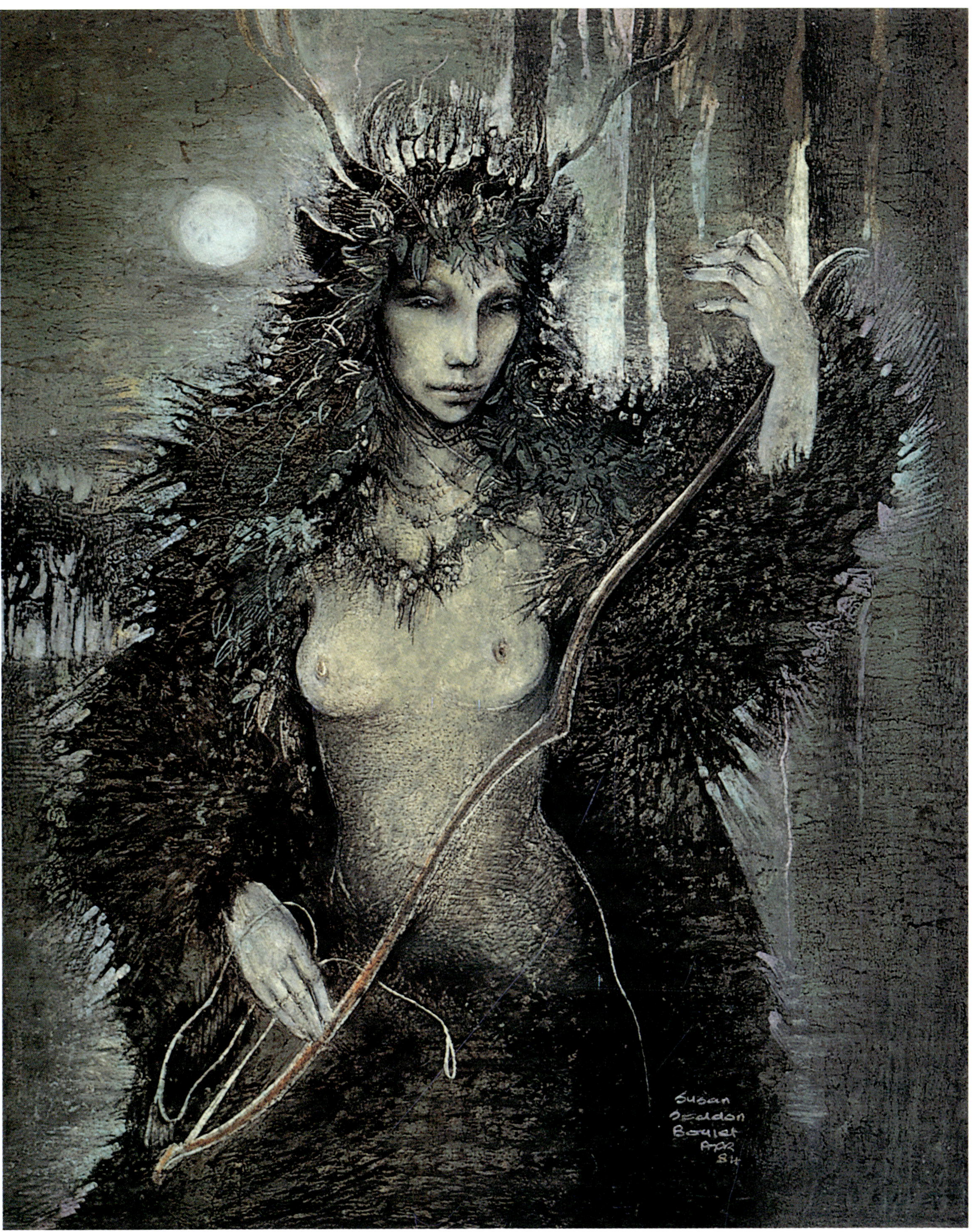
Susan
Seddon
Boulet
APR
84

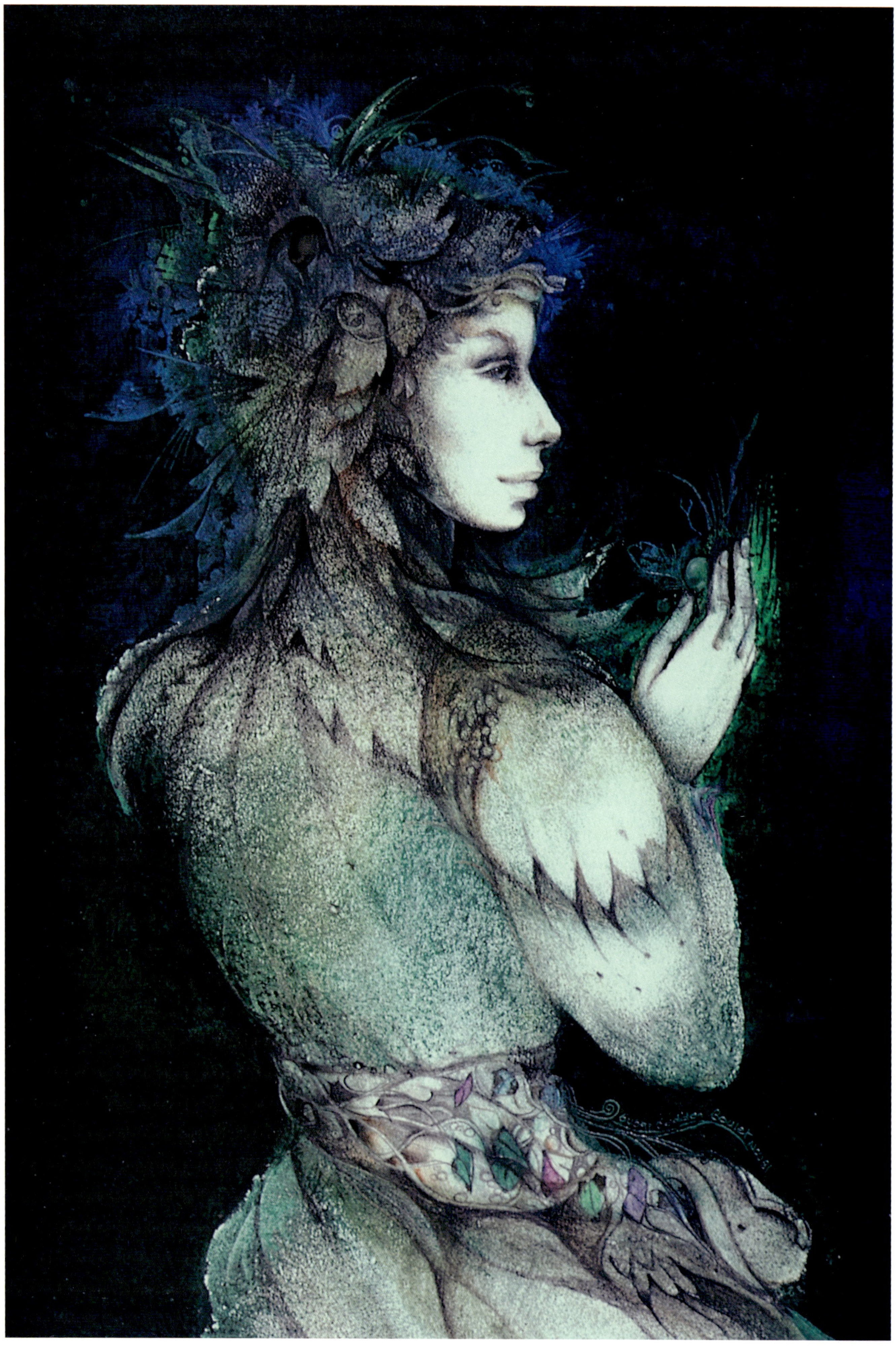

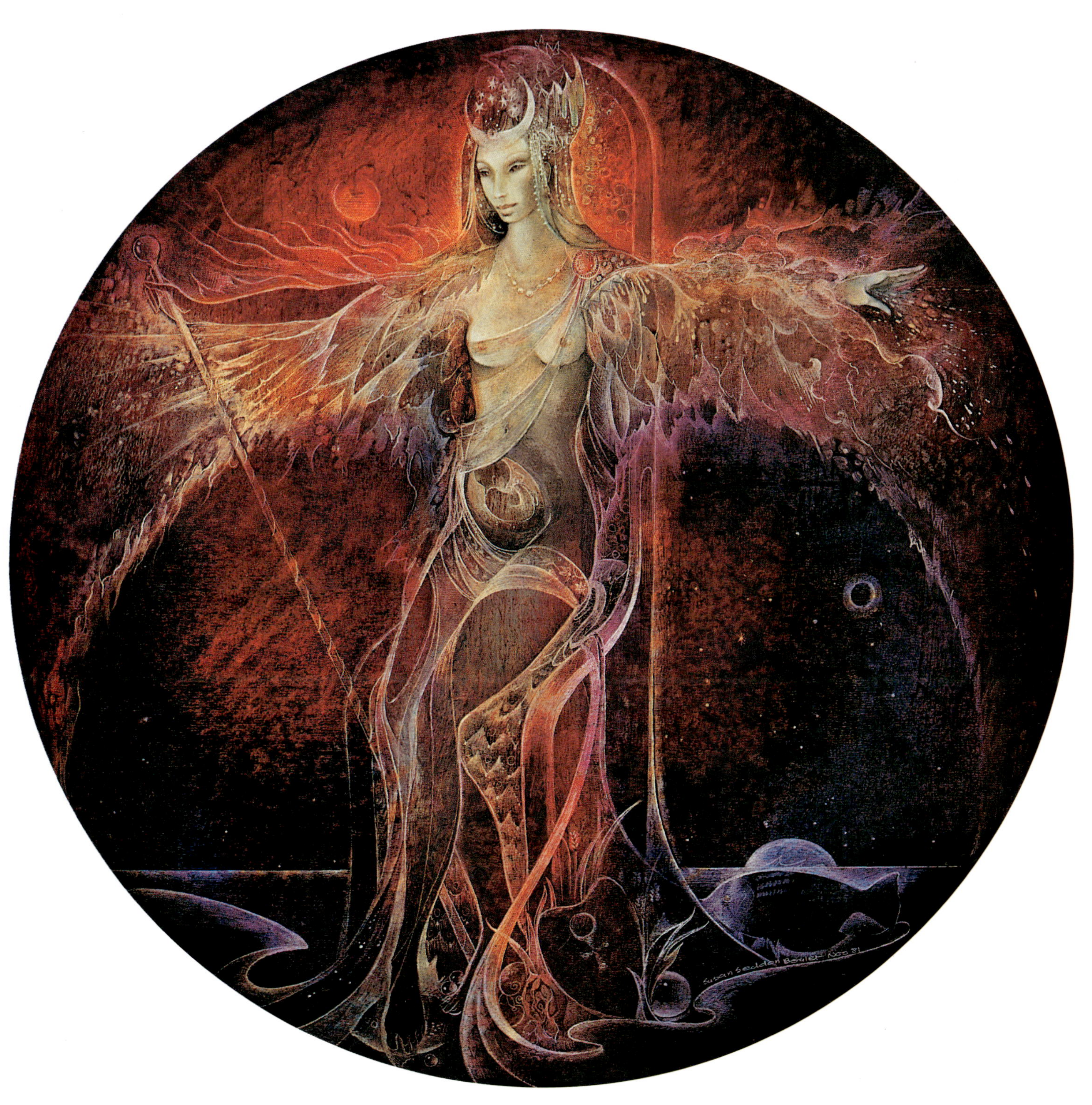
Susan Seddon Boulet Nov 81

Eurydice

Eurydice appears in Greek myth as the wife of the singer Orpheus. She is, in fact, the moon-goddess ruler of the underworld, a Great Goddess of creation and death. Her name means "wide justice," and she is "Eury-Dike," or Universal Justice, represented by the ever-turning wheel of fortune. As an underworld goddess, she, like Persephone, oversees both vegetative fertility and death. Here death is not the enemy but the regenerative necessity for life: to die is to return to the womb of the mother to be reborn. Eurydice is feminine energy as transformative energy: she gives birth to souls, recognizing that black is the color of fertility and that all life begins in darkness. To embrace Eurydice is to accept our hidden, dark side as the path to healing and wholeness.

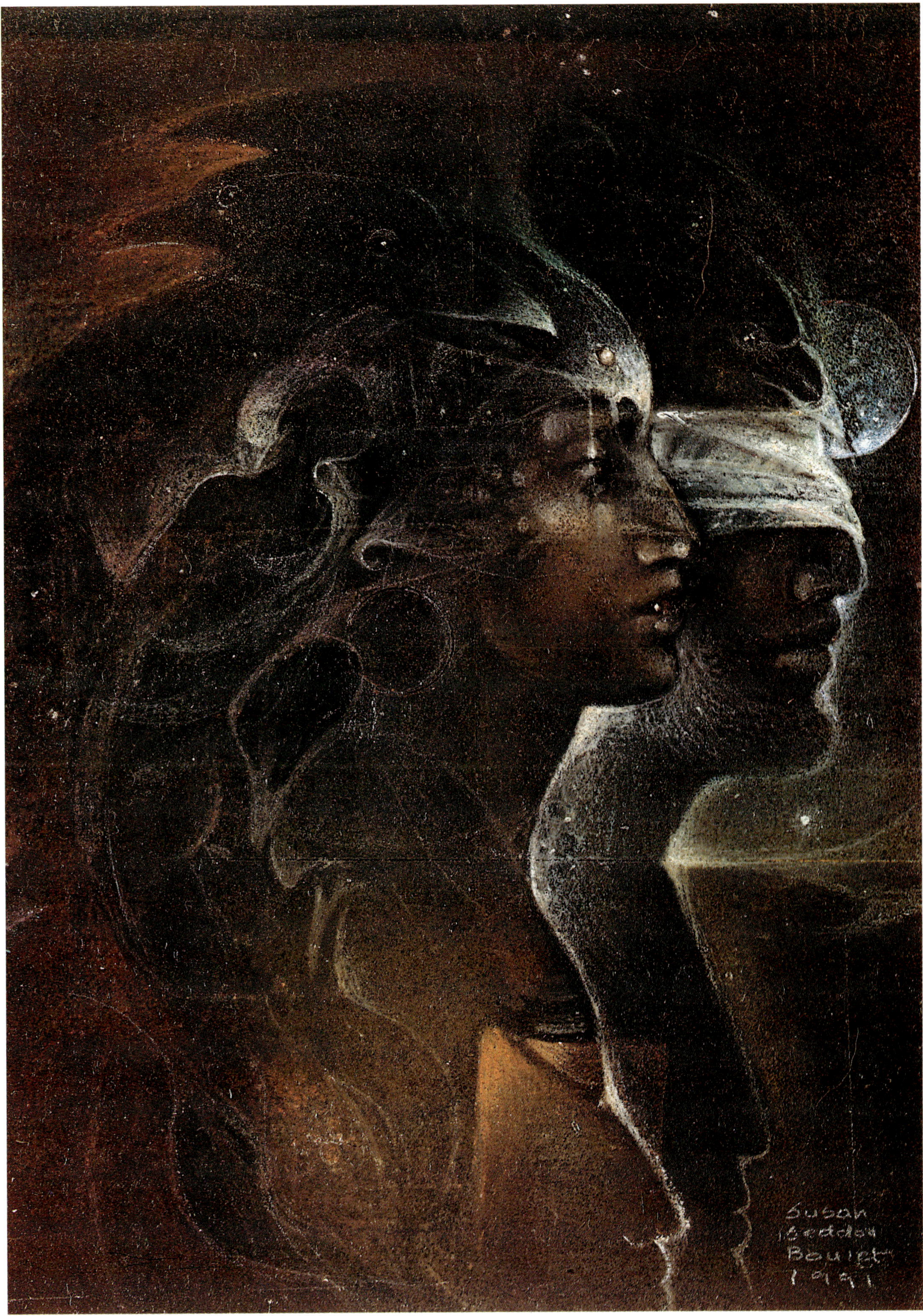
Susan
Seddon
Boulet
1991

Eve

The word *eve* means life; the goddess Eve is the mother and nurturer of all life. She is the creator of the world and of all living beings, the Lady of the Beasts and steward of all growing things. Even in the Bible she is portrayed with a snake, a potent symbol of the vital life force found in every living being, representing rebirth and regeneration. In one of the Gnostic texts it is Eve who calls Adam to life. Eve is the embodiment of primal female creative energy, of the powerful urge to create and sustain life. She is active femininity and relatedness to all that lives. She is life itself.

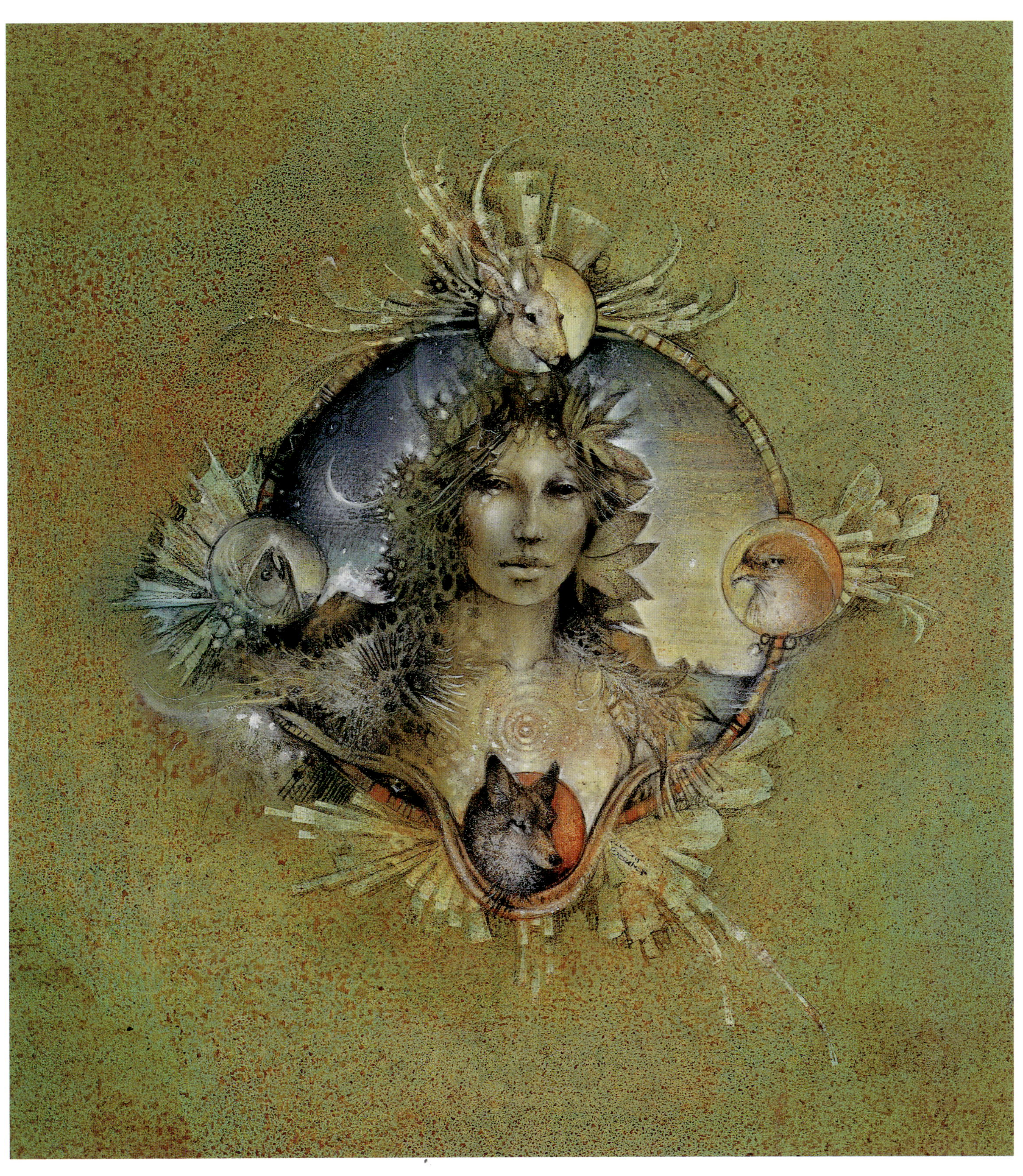

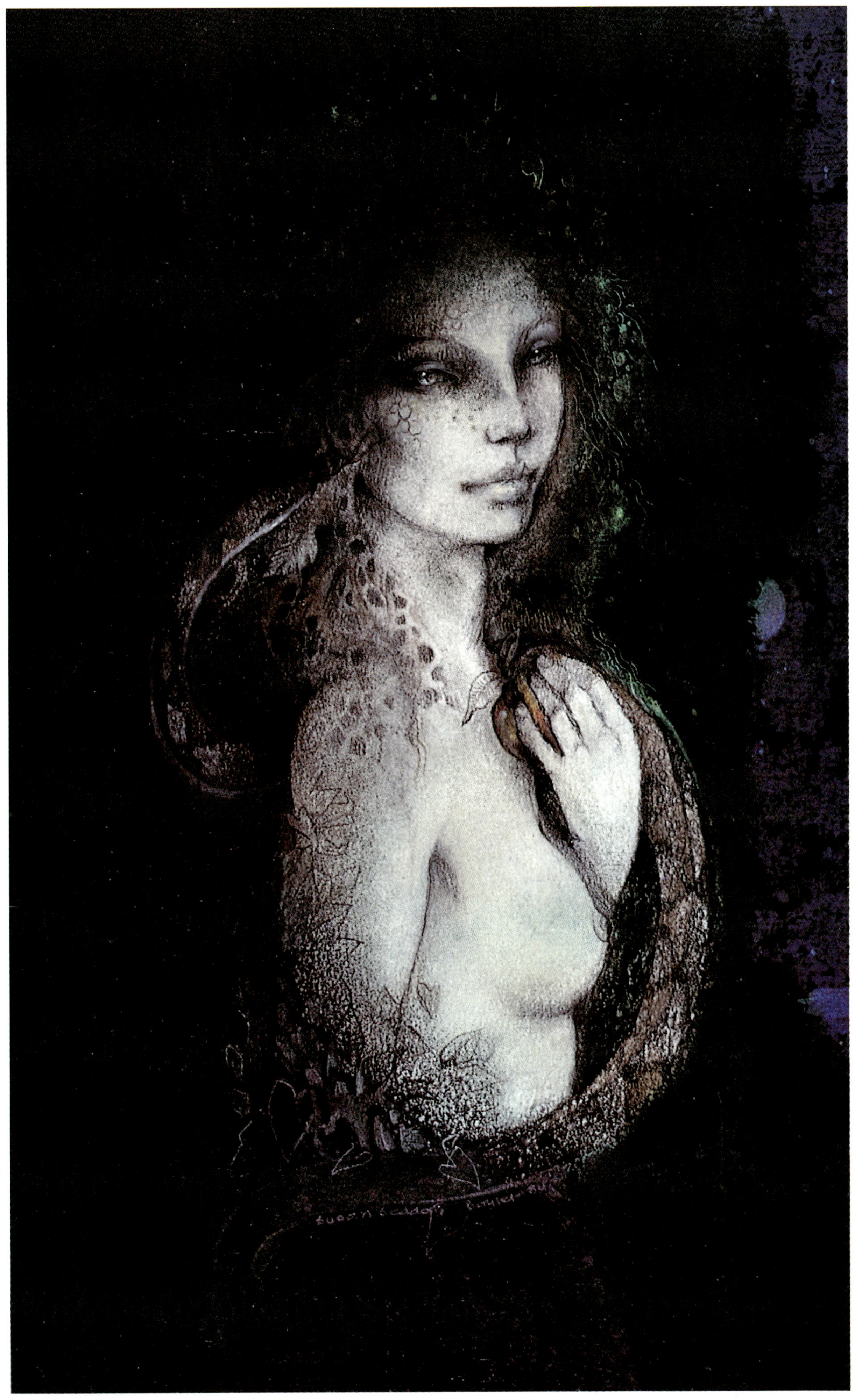

Gaia

Gaia existed before everything; she existed before time. Gaia, the eternal, prehistoric earth mother goddess, is fertility incarnate, moist, mysterious, strong. She is life energy itself; everything that lives, breathing or not, overflows with her life. She is the earth and all the powers of the earth. Gaia is not always a consoling goddess: standing for life and generation without thought of consequence, she has an energy and a power that must be approached carefully. All bodies eventually return to her, into the black, fertile earth, to be devoured and to receive her life to live again.

Gaia was the original deity at Delphi, for she is the giver of dreams, mantic oracles and prophecies. As goddess of the soul, she reminds us that the soul develops in dark places and that ultimately soul must be rooted in body, in earth. She is a reminder that we must ground ourselves in the reality of nature and incorporate all sides of ourselves, be they pleasant or unpleasant, light or dark.

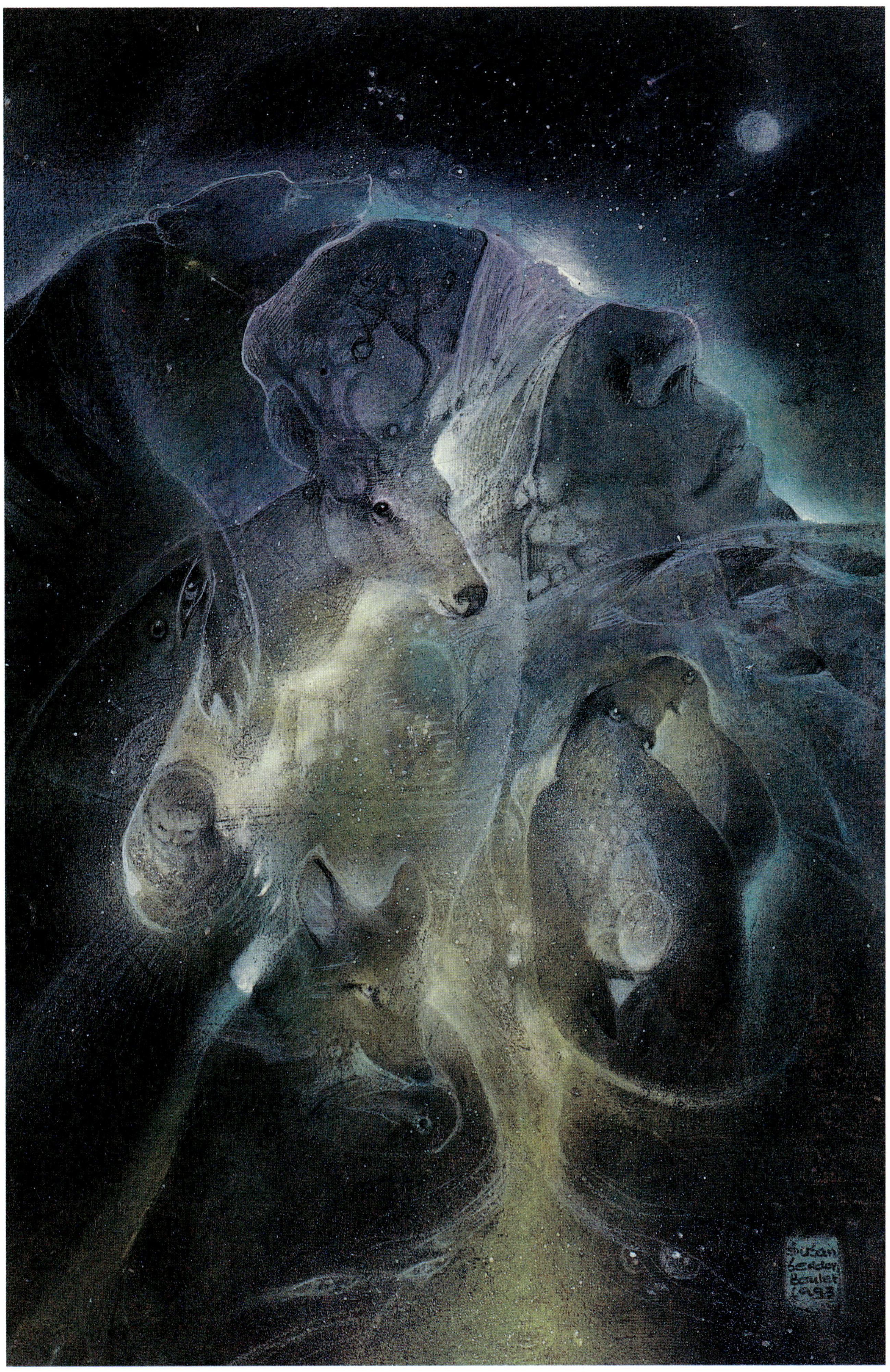
Susan
Seddon
Boulet
1993

Guinevere

From very early times, the Great Goddess has been a trinity: her three faces are typically virgin, mother and crone. Guinevere (in Welsh, Gwenhyfar) is the ancient Welsh Triple Goddess, the goddess of dawn and spring. Her ancient role is echoed in the version of the Arthurian legends in which King Arthur marries three women, each named Guinevere, and in the Celtic tradition that in order to be king a man must marry the goddess. Guinevere means "white waves," white being the traditional color of the virgin. Here "virgin" means what Esther Harding calls "One-in-Herself," referring to a woman or goddess who is complete in and of herself. Waves associate Guinevere with the regenerative power of the sea. As queen she is the eternal feminine principle of strength and order in a peaceful universe.

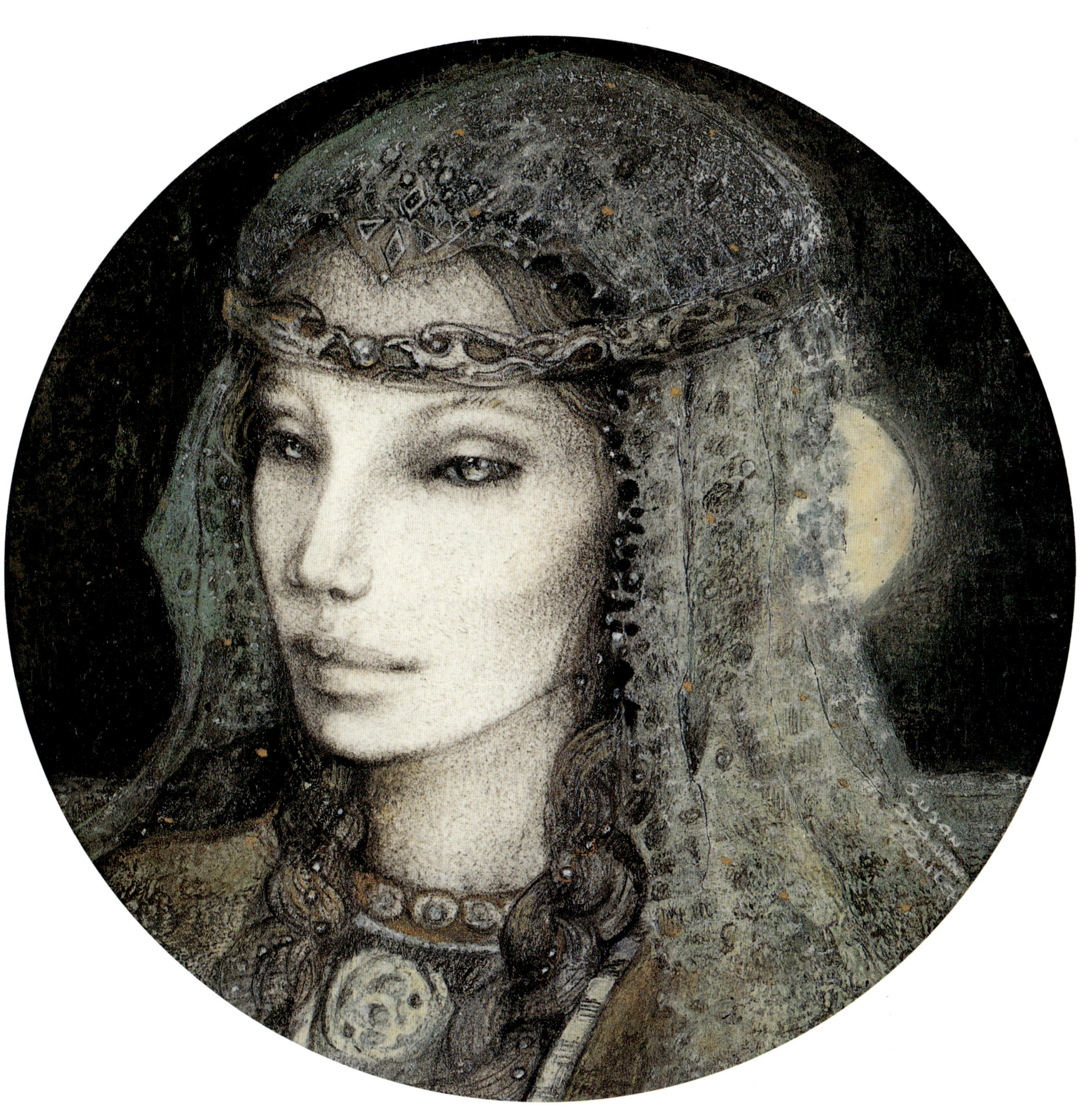

Hebe

Hebe's name literally means "youth." She is the maiden form of Hipta, the earth mother, and possibly is the same as Hawwa, the mother of all living things. In early myth she is also called Ganymeda, the Brilliant. She is a spring goddess, everlastingly youthful and beautiful, a goddess of the dawn. An incarnation of all that is young and fresh, she is maiden youth in its first bloom. Her ancient grove was a sanctuary for slaves and thieves.

In Greek mythology she is sometimes seen as young Hera, the queen of Olympus. Hebe is the original cupbearer to the gods and goddesses of Olympus; it is her nectar, the ambrosia of immortal youth, that keeps the deities everlastingly young. Thus the holy cup or vessel of the goddess dispenses the magic energy that renews life force and vitality. Hebe represents that part of us that is always young, always fresh and excited by life.

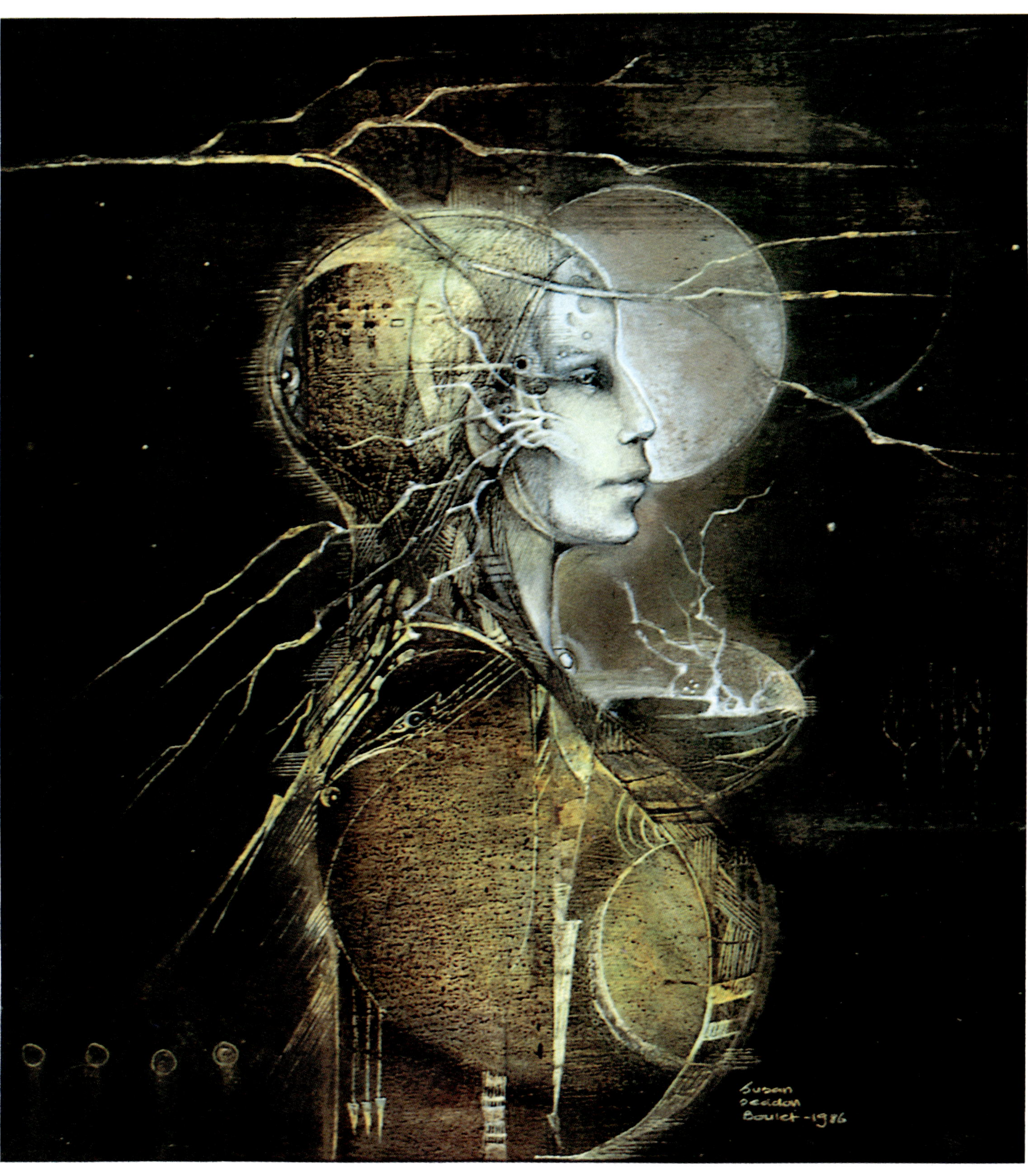
Susan
Seddon
Boulet-1986

Hel

Hel is the Norse queen of the underworld, a mother goddess in her underworld guise. She rules over a fiery womb of regeneration and is especially responsible for those who die of disease or old age. Her underworld, unlike the Christian hell, which received its name from her, is simply an otherworld, a place of renewal rather than a place of punishment and misery. When northern shamans visit her realm, they put on a *helkappe*, a magic mask (sometimes a helmet) that renders them invisible. It is possible that the masked harlequin, a standard character in commedia dell'arte, was originally one of the kindred of the goddess Hel. Hel is an embodiment of the divine mystery, a challenge to look behind the mask of appearances to see things as they really are.

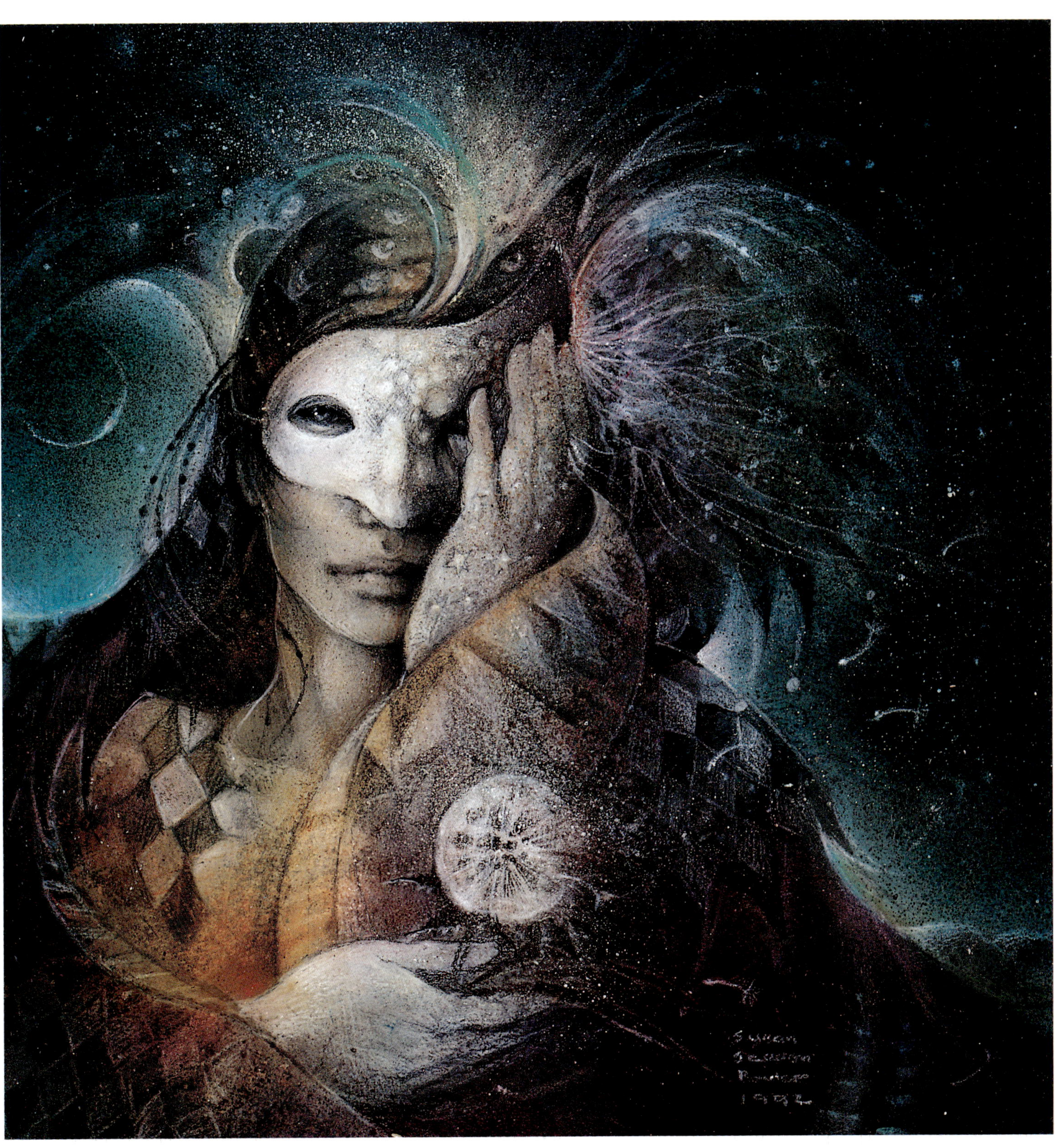

Hera

Hera is a very ancient goddess who, before she appeared as wife to Zeus in Greek mythology, was a powerful, matrilineal queen in her own right. Hera is the original all-powerful, multifunctional goddess responsible for every aspect of existence, a symbol of the complete woman. Among the Greeks, Hera was the goddess of marriage, a special goddess of women who accompanies each woman through every moment of her life. Her various titles point to her roles as bringer of fertility; goddess of marriage; protector of children, of women during childbirth and of money; and presider over all aspects of public life. She was often represented with a peacock, symbolic of beauty, luxury and immortality. The spots on its feathers reflect the starry firmament, and the peacock has knowledge of the weather, reflecting the ancient role of the goddess as bringer of the seasons. Hera is a mature, powerful goddess, combining both practicality and nurturing, a strong image of the supremacy of the queen within.

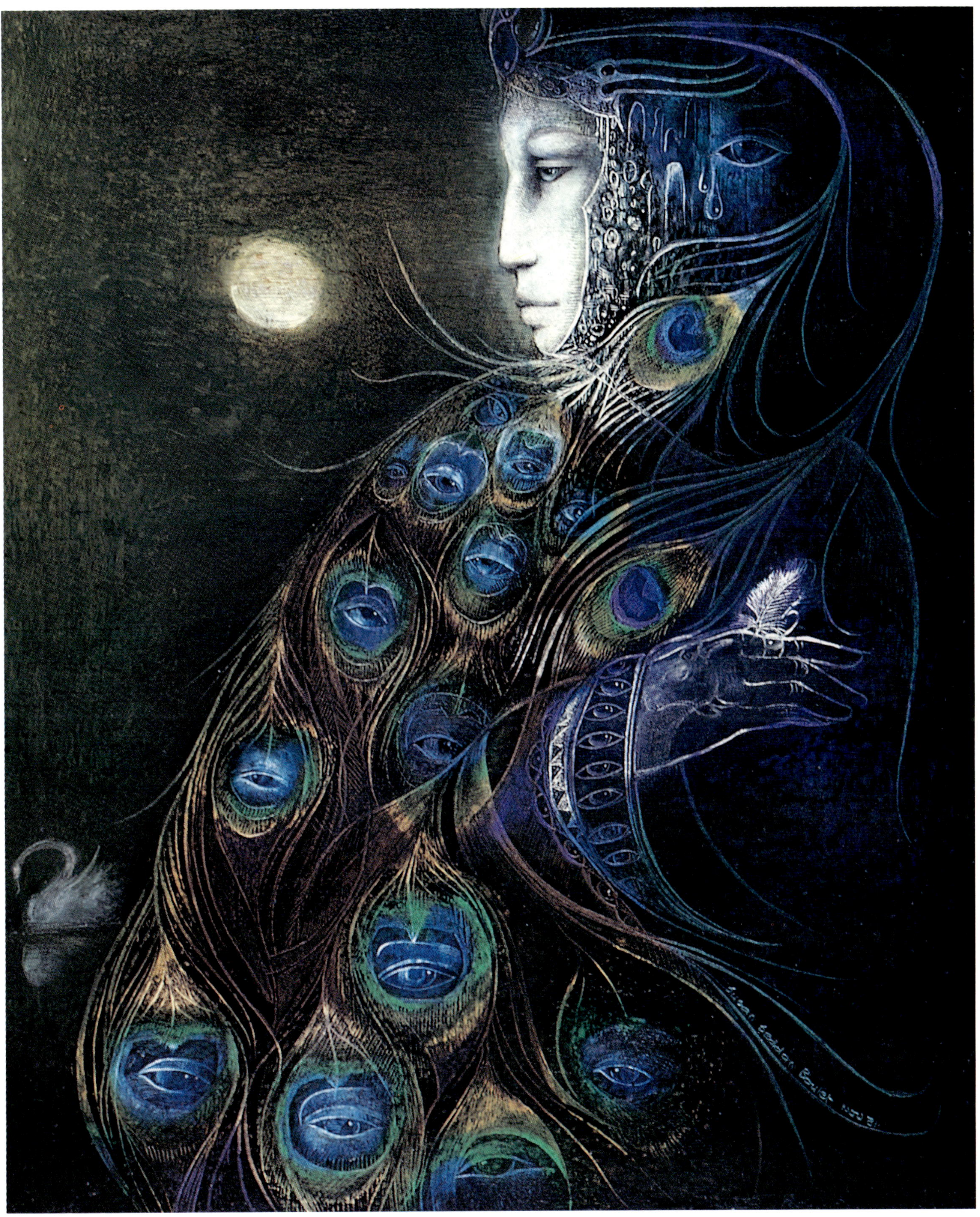

High Priestess

The priestess is the direct representative of the goddess on earth. She has direct responsibility for functions that ensure fertility and ongoing creation. Priestesses often were responsible for ensuring rain, for the goddess was the giver of dew and of rain. They often tended a sacred flame, the embodiment of the creative spark of life.

The High Priestess is the Great Goddess herself, a universal figure found in such diverse guises as Isis in Egypt, Kuan Yin throughout all of Asia, Athena in Greece and Rhiannon among the Celts. The goddess as High Priestess is a symbol of creativity, balance, intuition and, especially, wisdom. This goddess is all-knowing and all-wise; she creates life out of herself and bestows life-giving waters. At the proper time she takes life away so that the divine spark in each person may be freed to continue on its journey. The High Priestess is a reminder of the innate wisdom in each of us. She demands that we connect to the divine spark within and manifest it in the world.

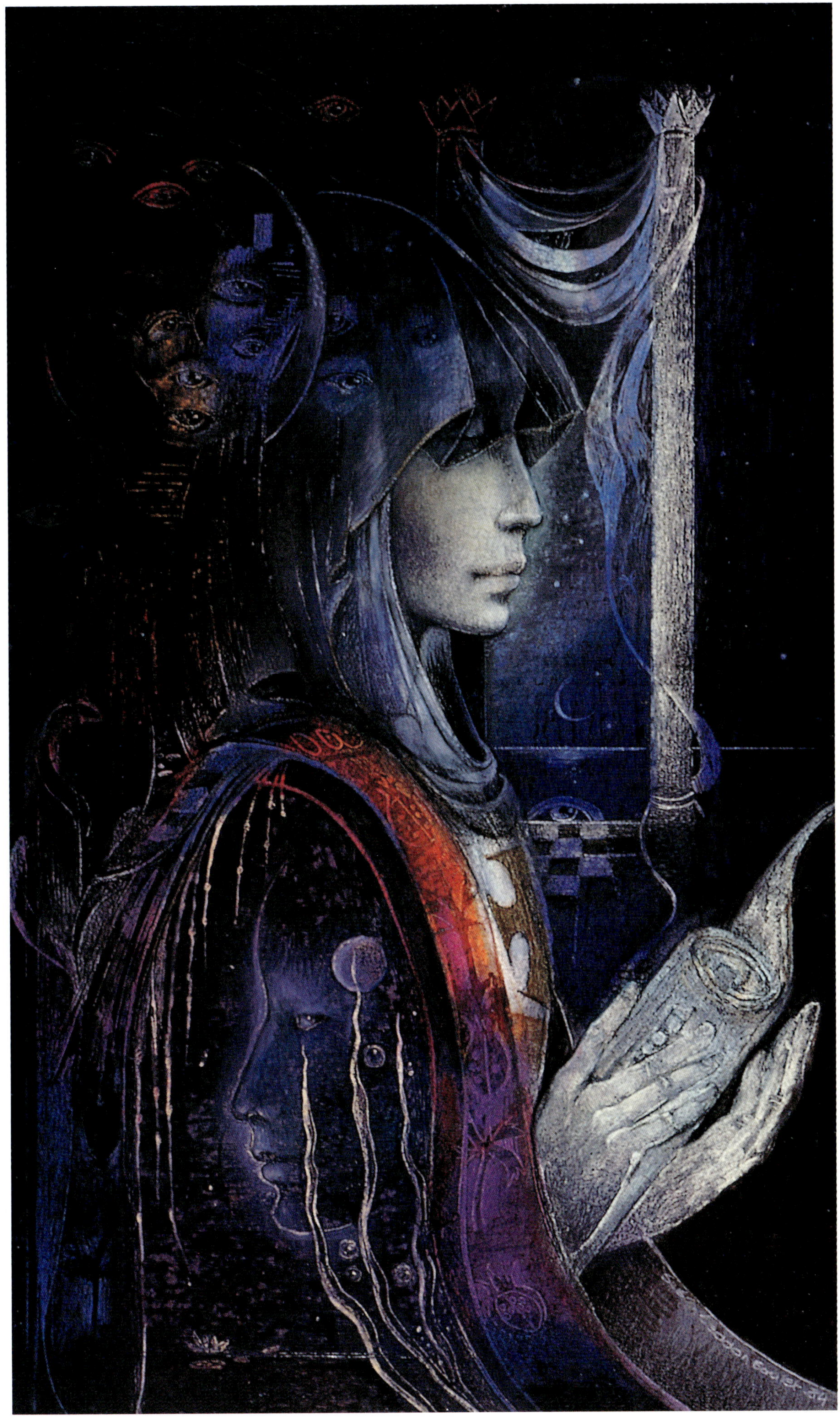

Inanna

Inanna is the ancient Sumerian mother goddess. Both the protector of grain and the queen of heaven, she combines earth and sky. Powerful, self-sufficient, passionate and many-sided, she is a fertility goddess as well as the source of the earth's wells, springs and rivers. Each year Inanna descends to the underworld to resurrect her consort, Dumuzi. At each of the seven gates she leaves one of her garments behind until, naked, she meets her sister Erishkigal, queen of the underworld. Erishkigal kills Inanna and hangs her on a hook until Inanna herself is resurrected and returns to life. Inanna is a representation of the many facets that go into being feminine as well as a guide into the dark places of psychological and spiritual death and disintegration.

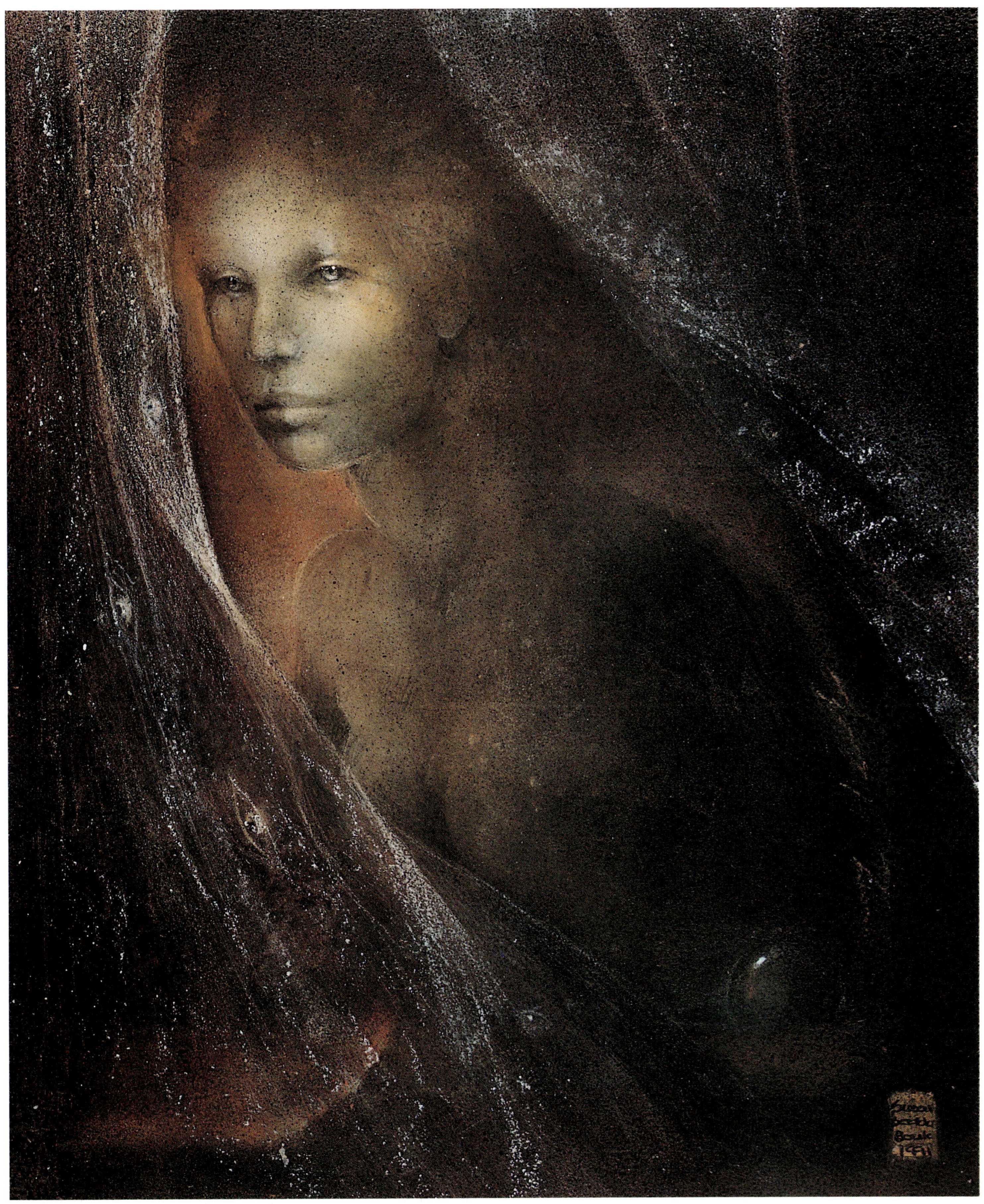

Ishtar

Ishtar is the multilayered Babylonian creator goddess, the source of all life and embodiment of the power of nature. She is the giver of plenty, a lawgiver, a judge, the goddess of time as well as the goddess of both love and war. Her name means "giver of light" and derives from her role as queen of heaven. She is the planet Venus as both morning and evening star, and her girdle is the zodiacal belt. Ishtar descends to the underworld and restores the vegetation god, Tammuz, to life and thus restores fertility to the earth. As she descends she removes a veil at each gate. While she is underground all life on earth is depressed and nothing comes to life. Ishtar is a multifaceted, powerful symbol of a forthright mode of being that is unafraid to venture into the depths of the underworld. She represents the creative feminine, active and strong.

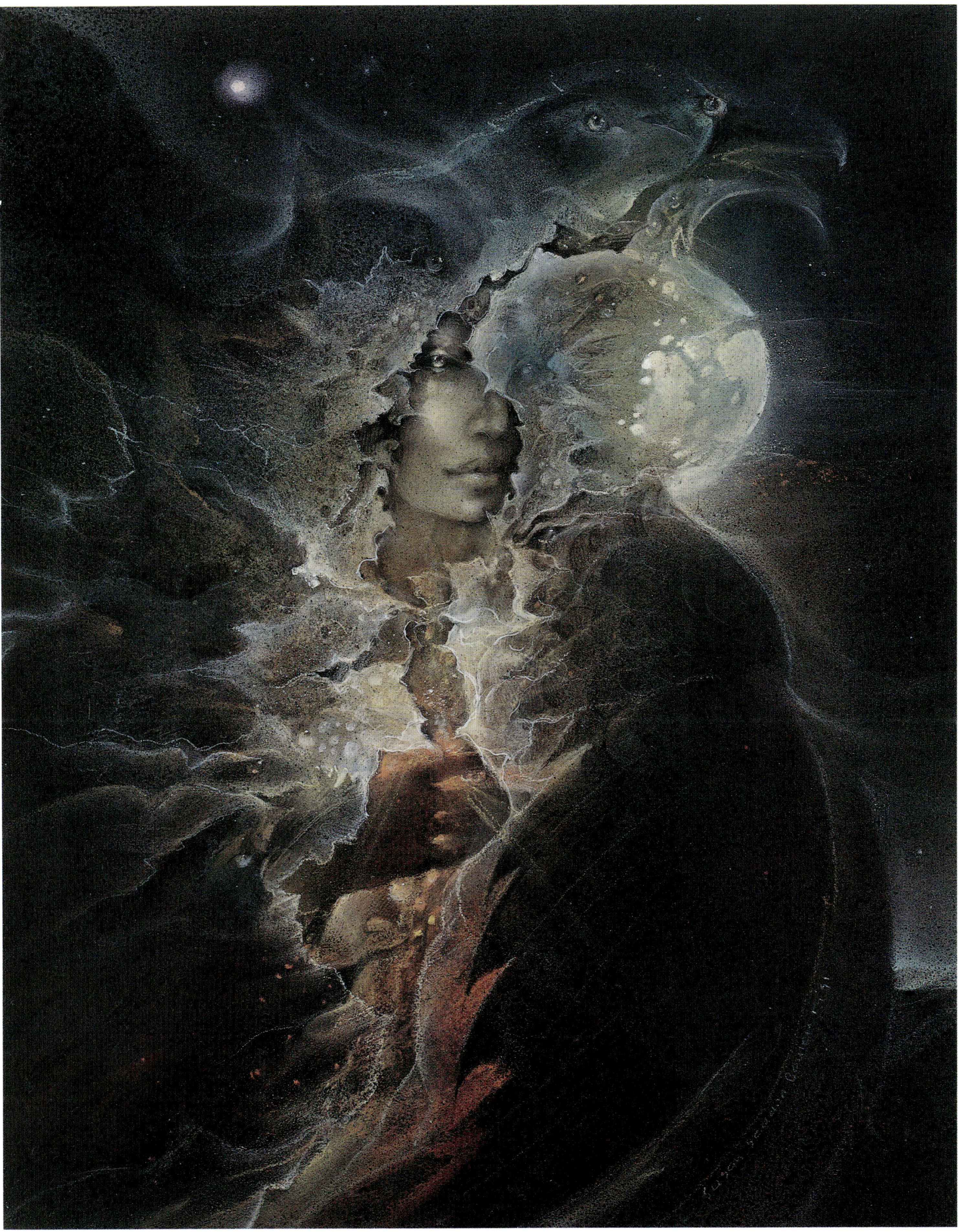

Isis and Osiris

In ancient Egypt Isis was among the oldest of goddesses, the mother and giver of all life. A moon goddess, she gives birth to the sun, creates and sustains all life and is the savior of all people. Some of her many names include Star of the Sea, Lady of the Beginning, Queen of Heaven and Mother of God. The teacher of agriculture, she is also the goddess of medicine and wisdom. The hieroglyph for her name is a throne because she is the throne from which the king arose or was born.

Osiris was her brother and husband. When Osiris was murdered by his brother Set, Isis searched for him. Finding him, she revived him and conceived their son, Horus. When Set again took Osiris and scattered his body in fourteen pieces, Isis hunted down each piece, except for his reproductive organs, which she was unable to locate, in order to give each piece a proper burial.

Isis is the universal goddess, representing total femininity. She can overcome death itself, yet she is not above grief: one of her tears, wept when Osiris was dying, caused the Nile River to flood. A wonderful image of the goddess's ability to give and to restore life, she underscores the depths of emotion that even a goddess must feel.

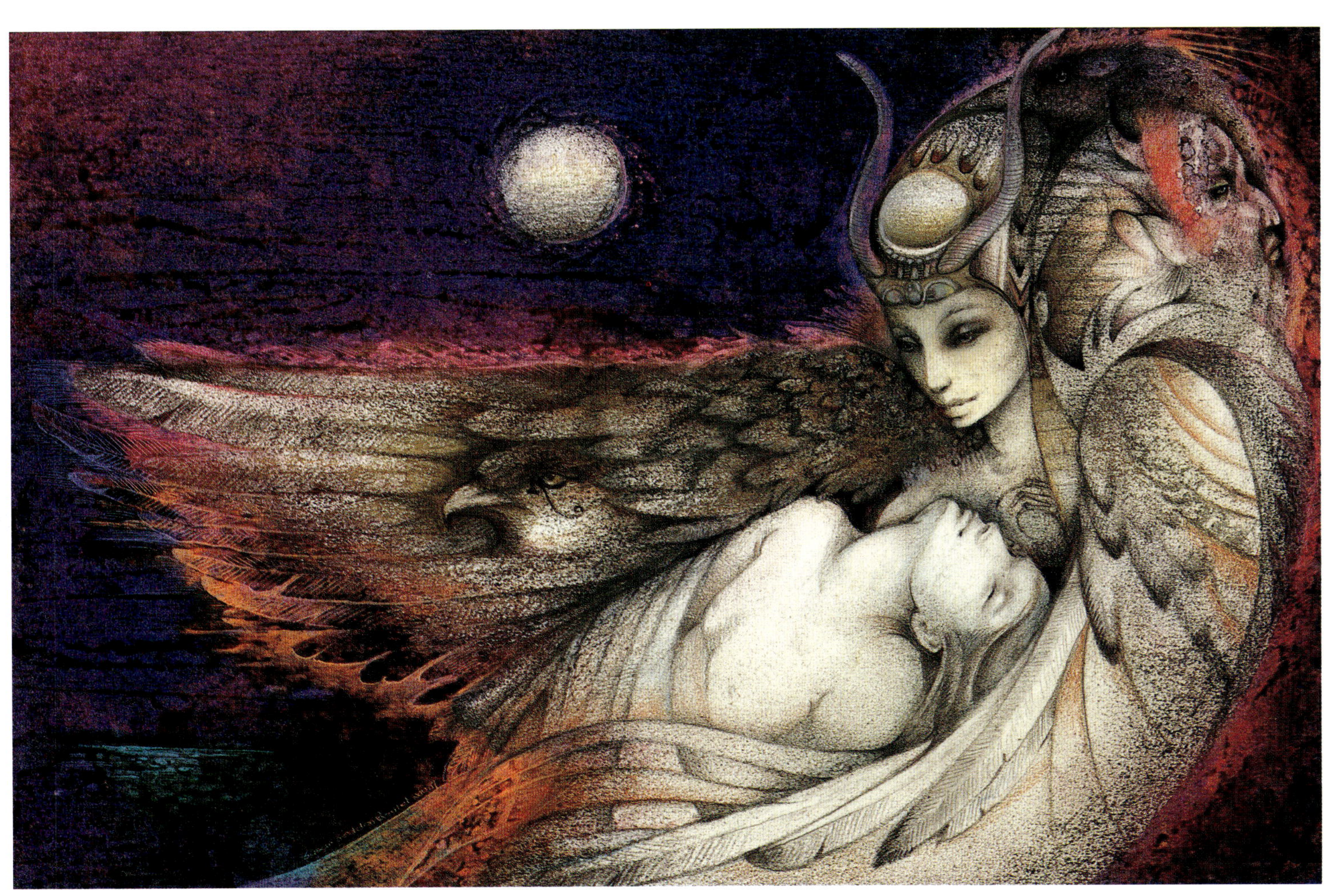

Ix Chel

Ix Chel is the ancient Mayan moon goddess who reigned supreme throughout the Yucatán Peninsula, in southern Mexico and as far south as El Salvador for more than a millennium. She is also called the Queen, Our Mother, the White Lady and the Goddess of Becoming. Although married to the sun, she is fiercely independent, allowing no one to own her: she remains free to come and go as she chooses. As a fertility goddess, she makes women fruitful and sends fertilizing rains to the earth. She is particularly honored as a patroness of childbirth and a healing goddess of medicine. Like many moon goddesses, she is the patroness of weaving. Ix Chel, like the waxing and waning moon, is comfortable with all sides of life. Her energy is midwife to our own creative ideas.

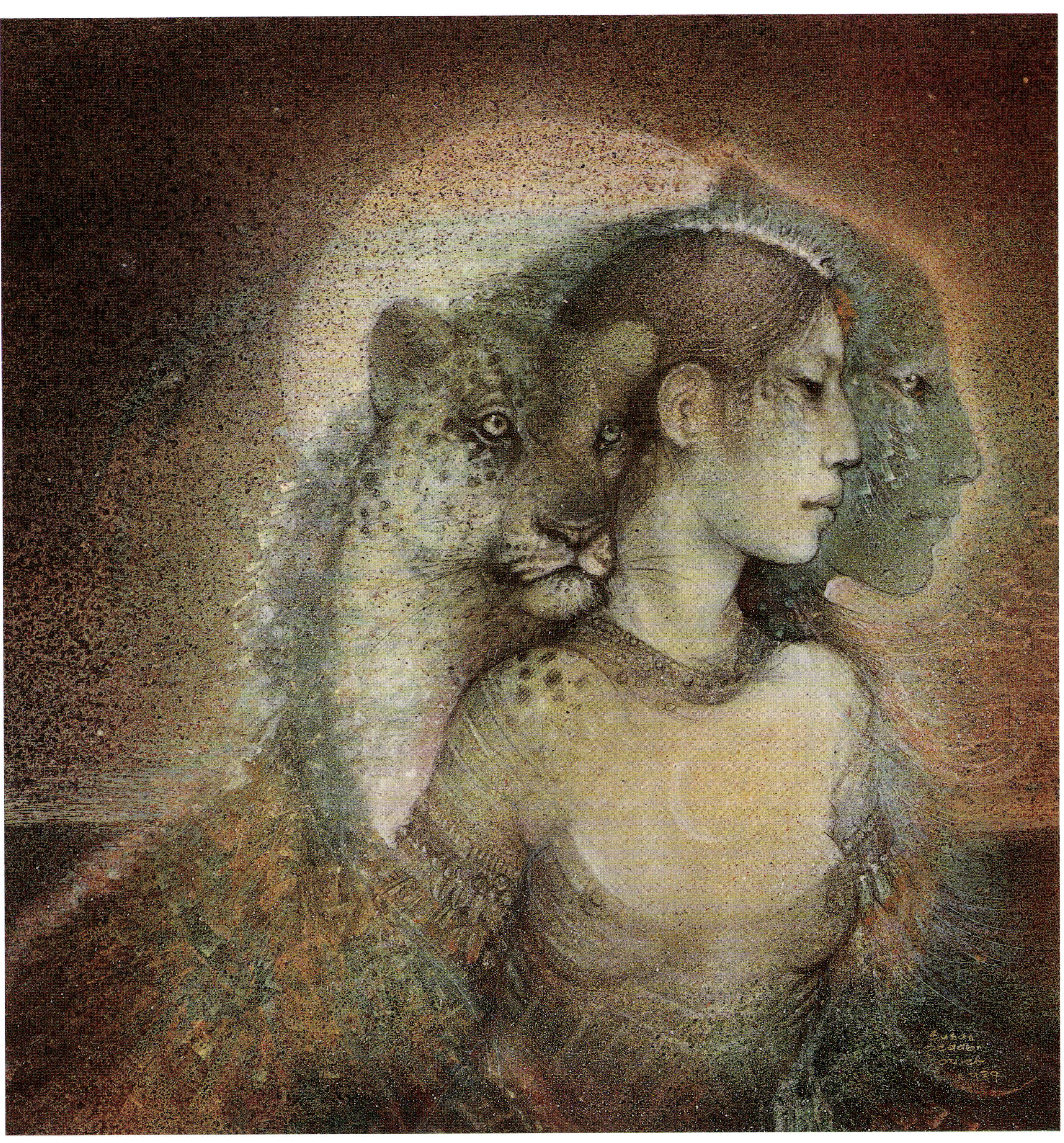

Kaltes

Kaltes is a moon goddess venerated by the Ugric peoples of western Siberia. A shape shifter, she is shown here manifested as a hare, an animal sacred to her. This appearance shows her lunar nature, for the hare is a lunar creature; many cultures, when looking at the moon, see the outline of the hare, who lives in the moon. The hare is often seen as an intermediary between lunar deities and humans, so the appearance of Kaltes in this form indicates her accessibility to her people.

Kaltes is known as a fertility goddess and a goddess of rejuvenation. She is called upon by women in childbirth, for she is especially venerated as a promoter of the beginning of the life cycle. Although she is somewhat feared because she can determine people's destinies, she is mostly revered for her gentle wisdom. She is a compassionate guide to the mysteries of life.

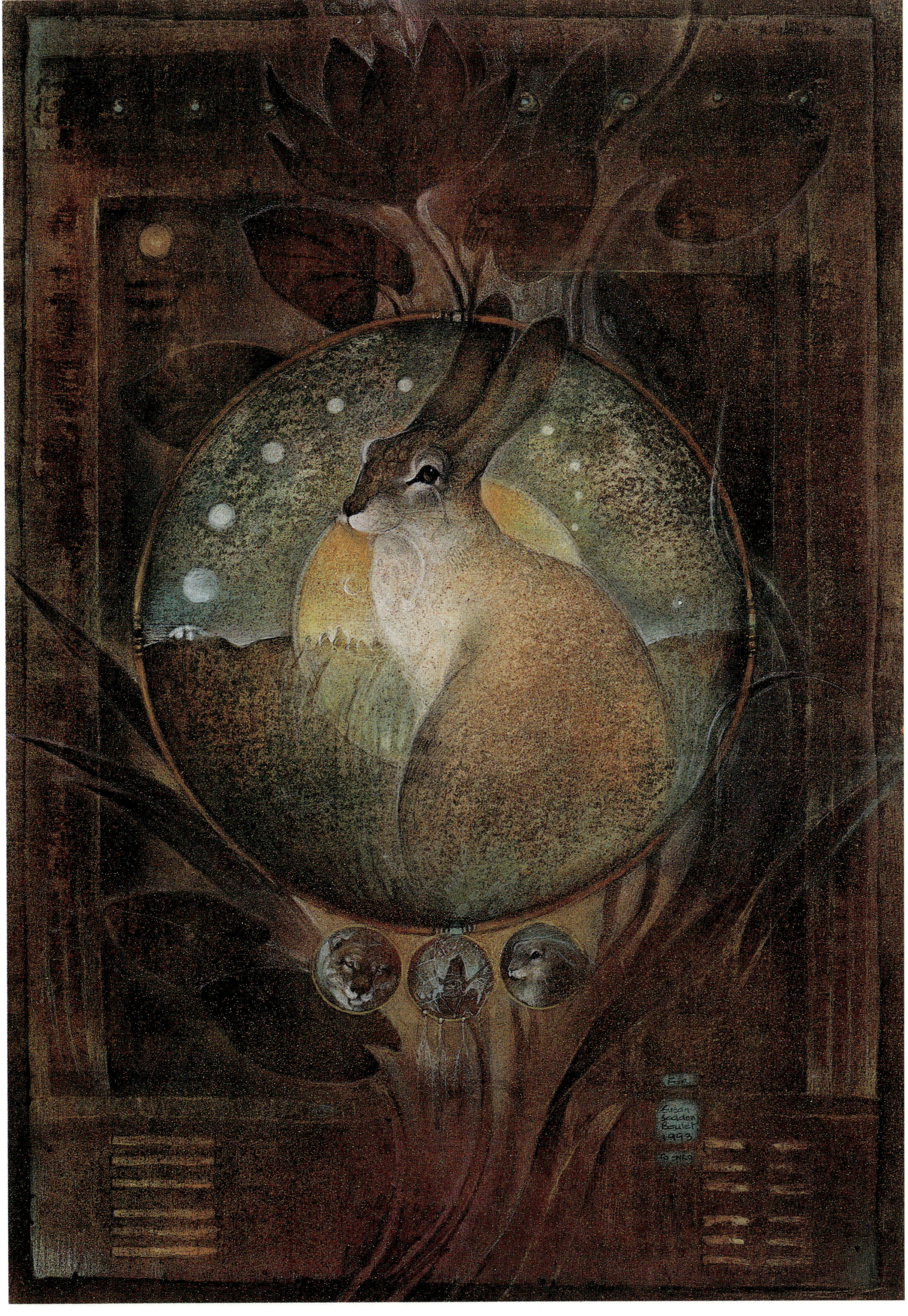

Lady of the Lake

As in many traditions in which a goddess bestows kingship, the Lady of the Lake, a mysterious Celtic goddess, gave King Arthur the sword Excalibur and thus established his power and his right to be king. Before he died, Arthur restored the sword to her, and it now remains with her beneath the waters of the deep. Sometimes named Vivien, in various traditions the Lady of the Lake is said to be one of several other goddesses. Nimuë was the sorceress who enchanted Merlin and placed him into a deep sleep. Morgan le Fay is a great queen death goddess and controller of fate. Rhiannon is a Welsh Great Goddess, a source of inspiration and an embodiment of both life and death.

Water, the source of all life, has long been the domain of the goddess. Lakes represent both the source of creative power and the land of the dead, life giving and death or renewal being the two main functions of the goddess. Water indicates both consciousness and revelation. The Lady of the Lake is a guide to the mysterious realms of emotion and renewal, a source of immense creativity. She can give us the energy we need to rule our lives.

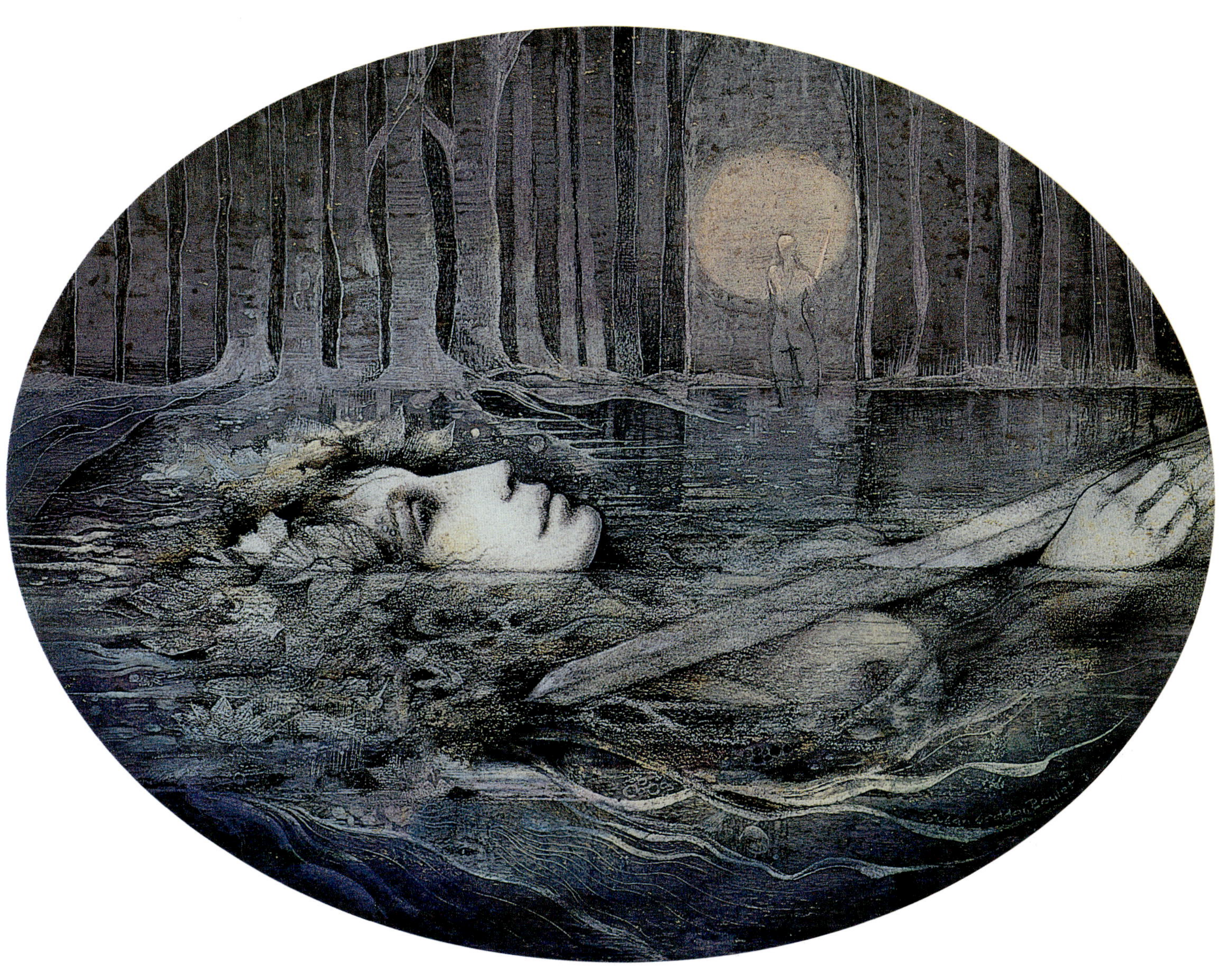

Lilith

Lilith is a Middle Eastern goddess of abundance, fertility and fecundity, the giver of agriculture to humans. The first woman created and the first wife of Adam, she refused to be subordinate to Adam in any way. Lilith is associated with the owl, a figure of darkness and deep wisdom, for she is also a goddess of death and transformation. She is sometimes represented as a demonic figure, for her dark wisdom and her sexual energy can be very threatening. She is known to appear as a frightening figure in dreams. Lilith is associated with the lotus, and the symbolism of that flower tells us much about her. The lotus, an exquisite flower that grows out of dark, rank, decaying earth, represents spiritual unfolding and the blossoming of the heart of wisdom. Like the lotus, Lilith challenges us to look upon our dark side and incorporate it into our wholeness so that our great beauty can blossom forth.

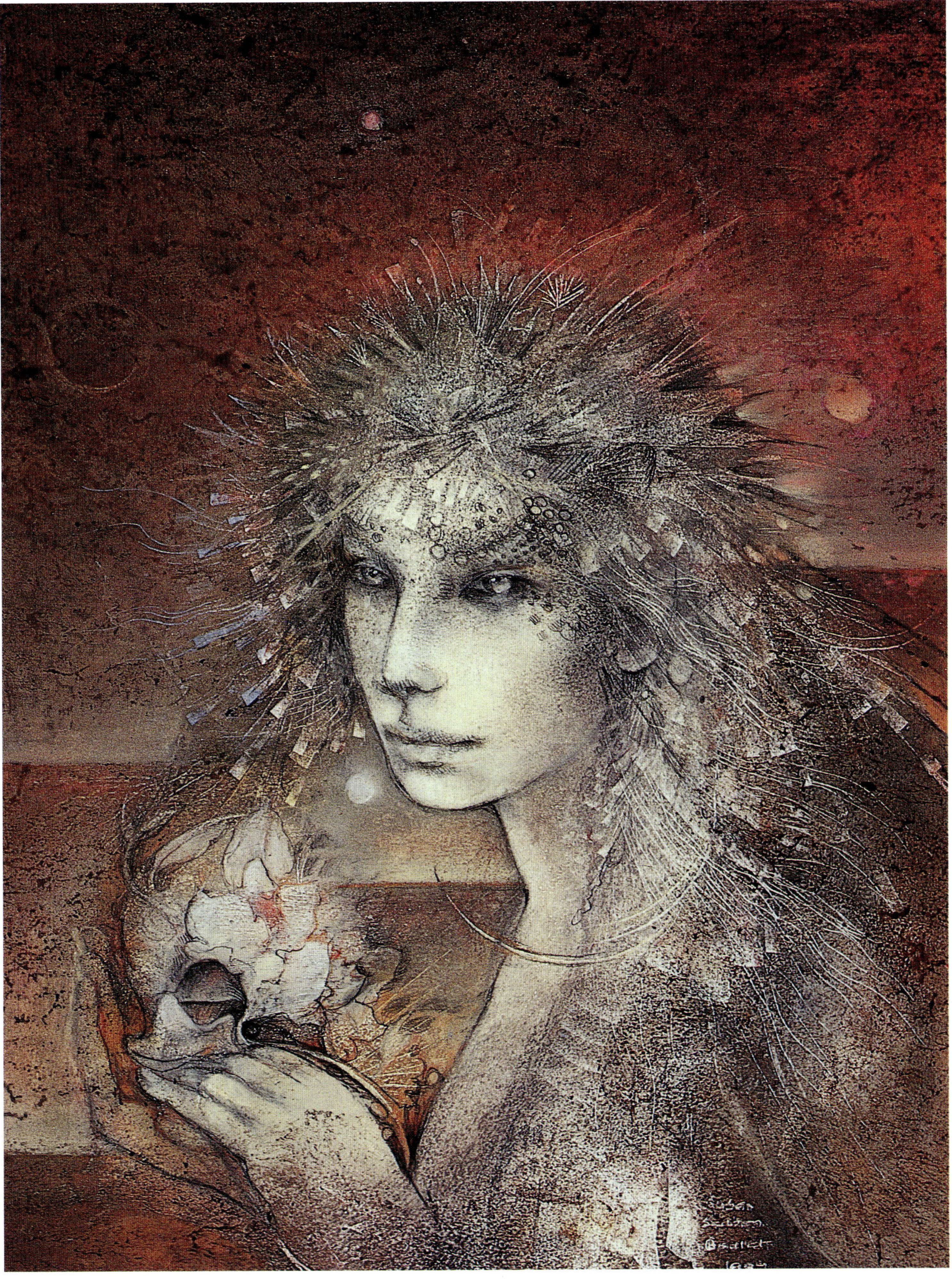

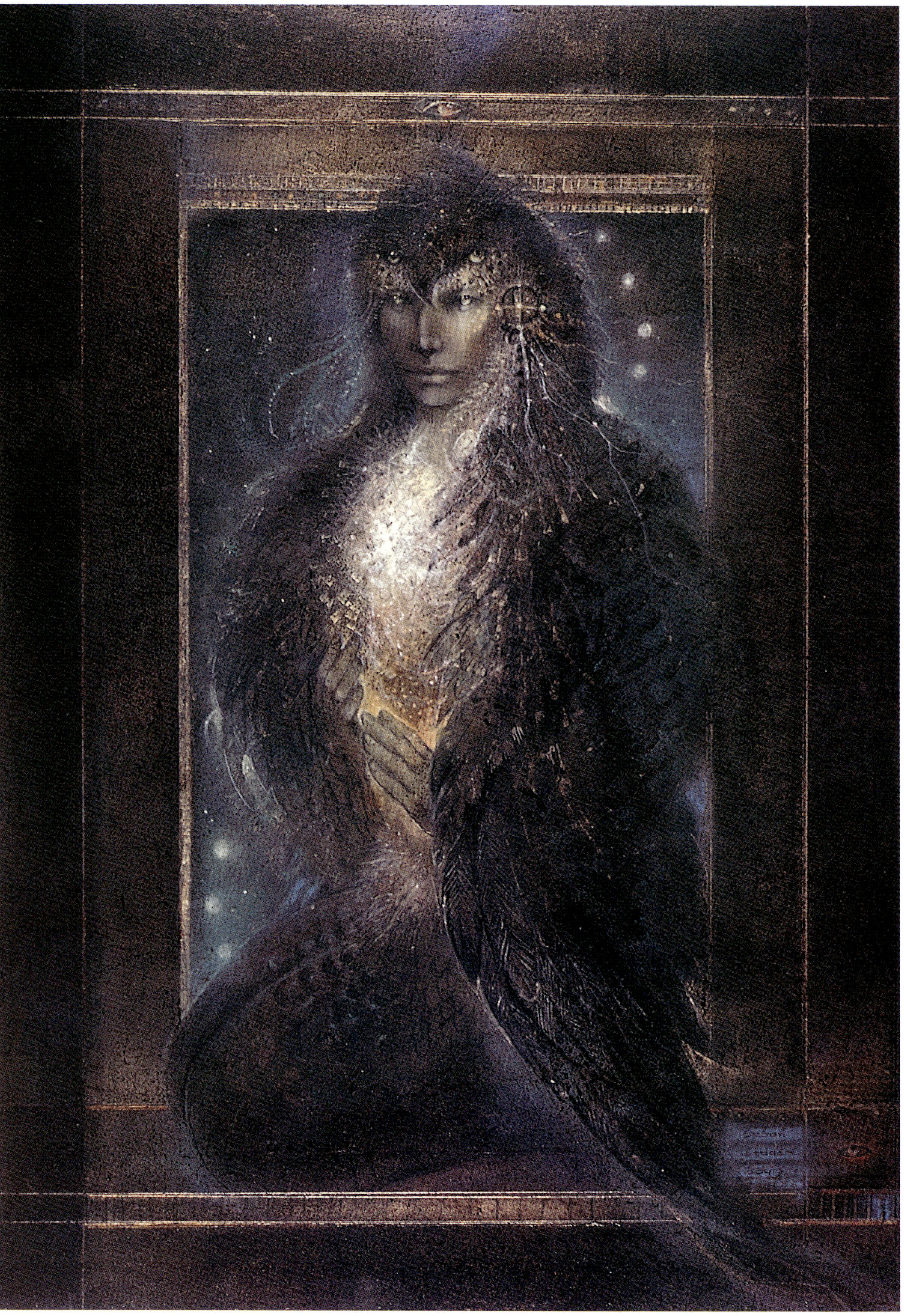

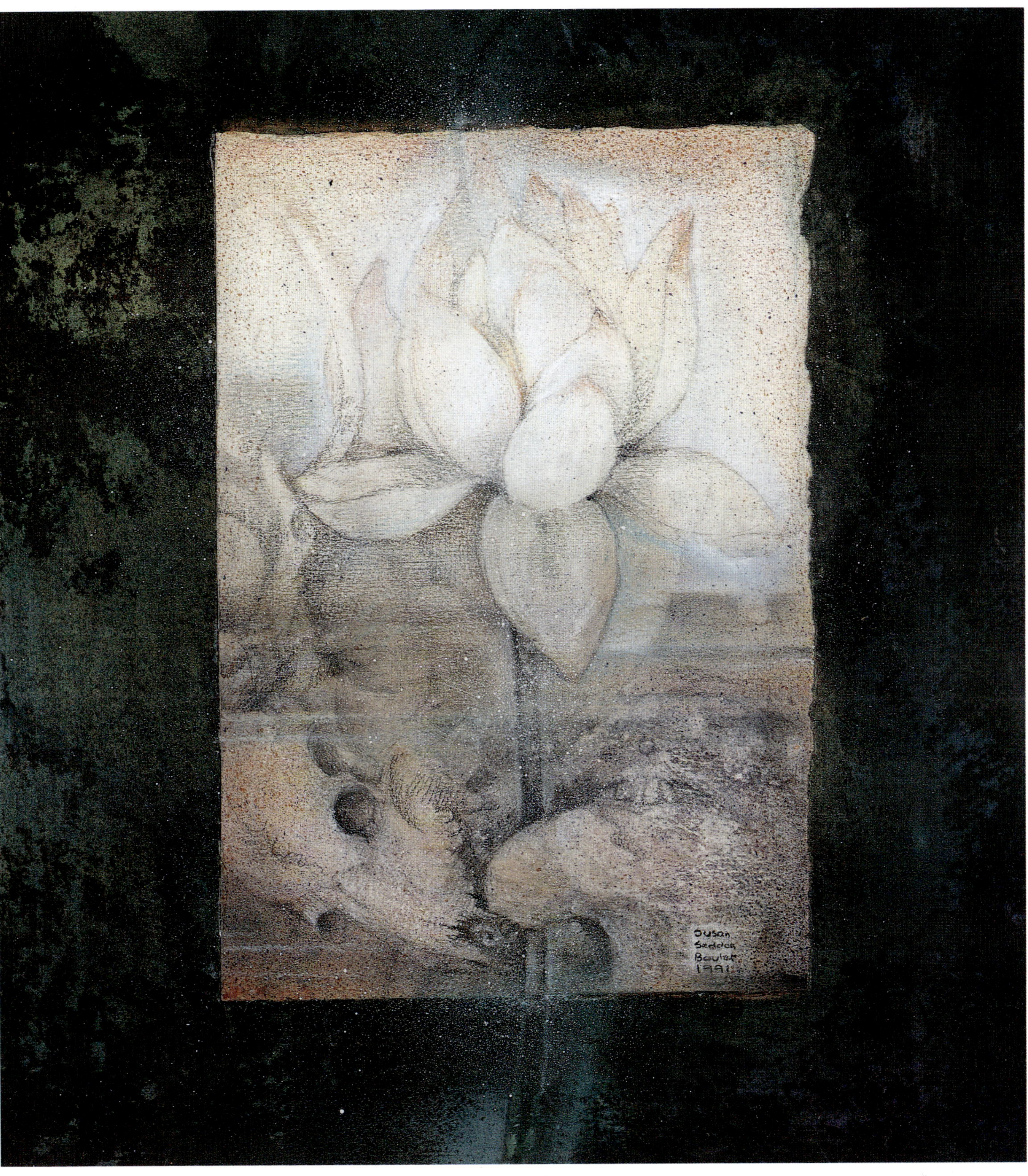
Susan
Seddon
Boulet
1991

Mary

The continued veneration of Mary, mother of Jesus, testifies to the power of the goddess and the need we have for her. Mary is most closely allied to the Middle Eastern moon goddesses; like them, she is a creator goddess. Associated with both the heavens and the sea or other waters, she is worshiped by Catholics as the Moon of the Church and as "Stella Maris," the Star of the Sea. The moment of the annunciation is when she confronts the truth of her own great creativity, symbolized by the angel of truth, Gabriel, made from fire. This is the moment at which she accepts the imperative to create, the need to bring forth life from the very center of her being. Mary is the goddess as womb, as source of all life and of regeneration. Mary is the original parthenogenetic goddess, who brings forth creation by herself, from herself. She is the mother of mercy and infinite compassion, the one we turn to in times of need. She is a reminder that compassion toward oneself fosters creativity; she reminds us to be gentle with ourselves.

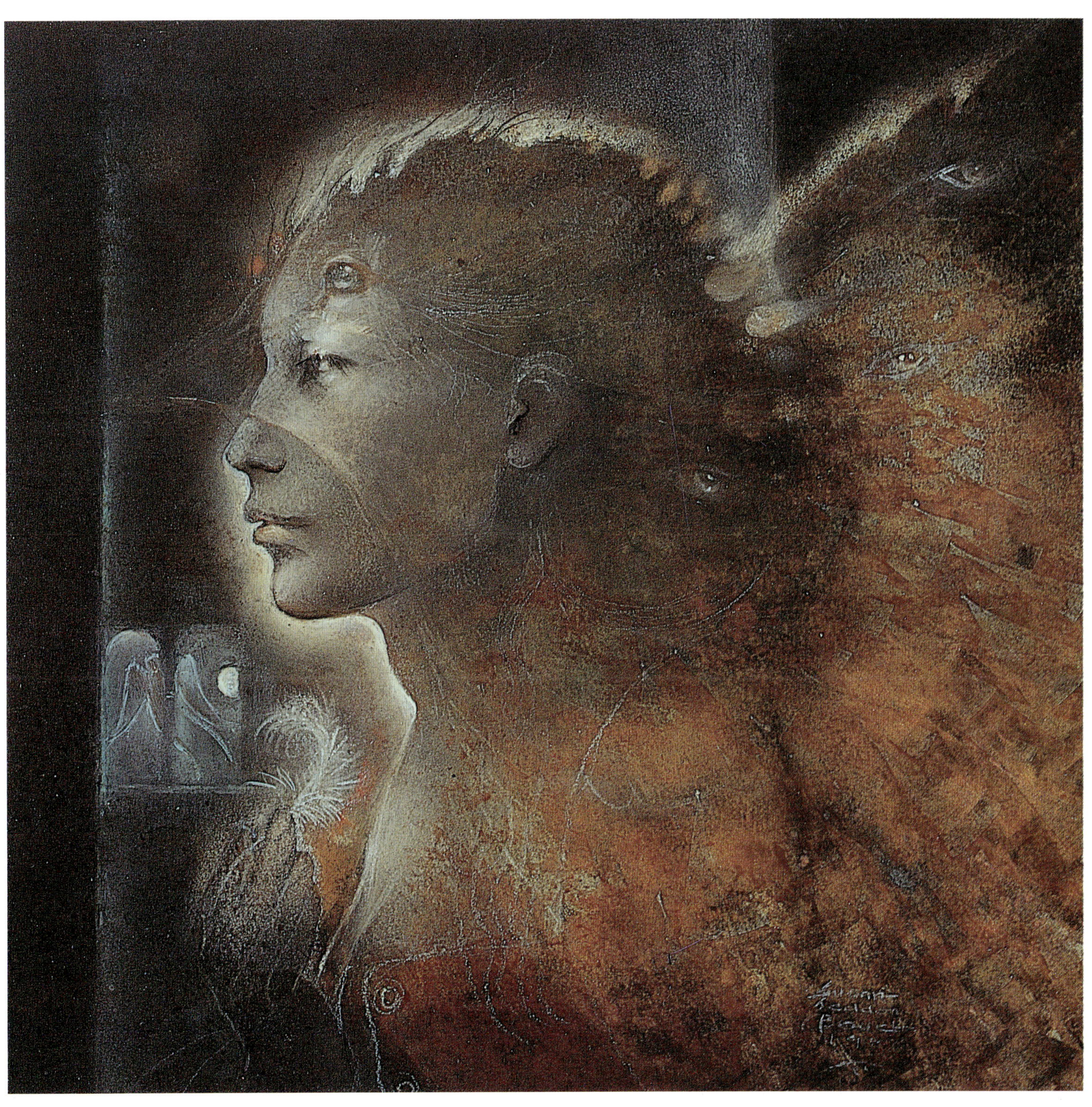

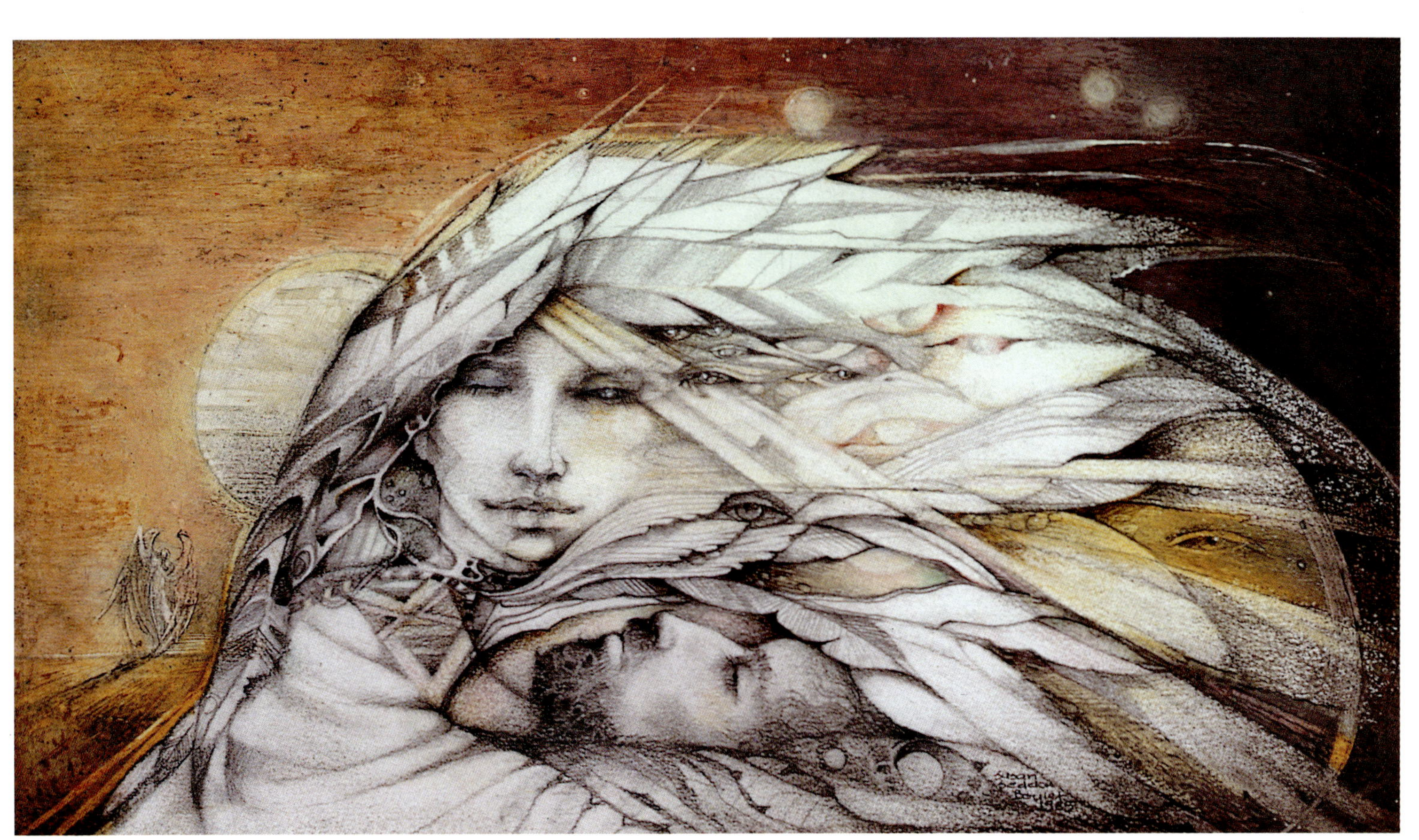

Medusa

When Medusa was slain, the horse Pegasus sprang forth from her blood. The Greeks portrayed Medusa as a horrifying Gorgon, an ugly woman with snakes for hair; anyone who looked at her face was turned to stone. And yet her name has the same root as *medicine* and *measure*, and derives from a Greek word meaning "to protect, to rule over."

Medusa is a moon goddess, the triple-headed Great Goddess in her death aspect. She is associated with blood, so to meet her is to meet the mysteries of moon-blood or menstrual blood, sacred and terrible, in many mythologies the source of all life. Medusa is serpent energy, enlivening, terrifying, impersonal. Somehow Medusa, a symbol of growth and generation that dies so that from death may come life, became a symbol of fear, for to look directly upon the divine is to face a terrifying reality. The blood from her slaying was used both to heal—even to restore life to the dead—and to kill.

Pegasus, the white horse who sprang from her blood, is instinct, wisdom, imagination, life force and intuitive understanding. From the hooves of Pegasus came the spring of Hippocrene, the source of the Muses' richest inspiration, the source of poetry.

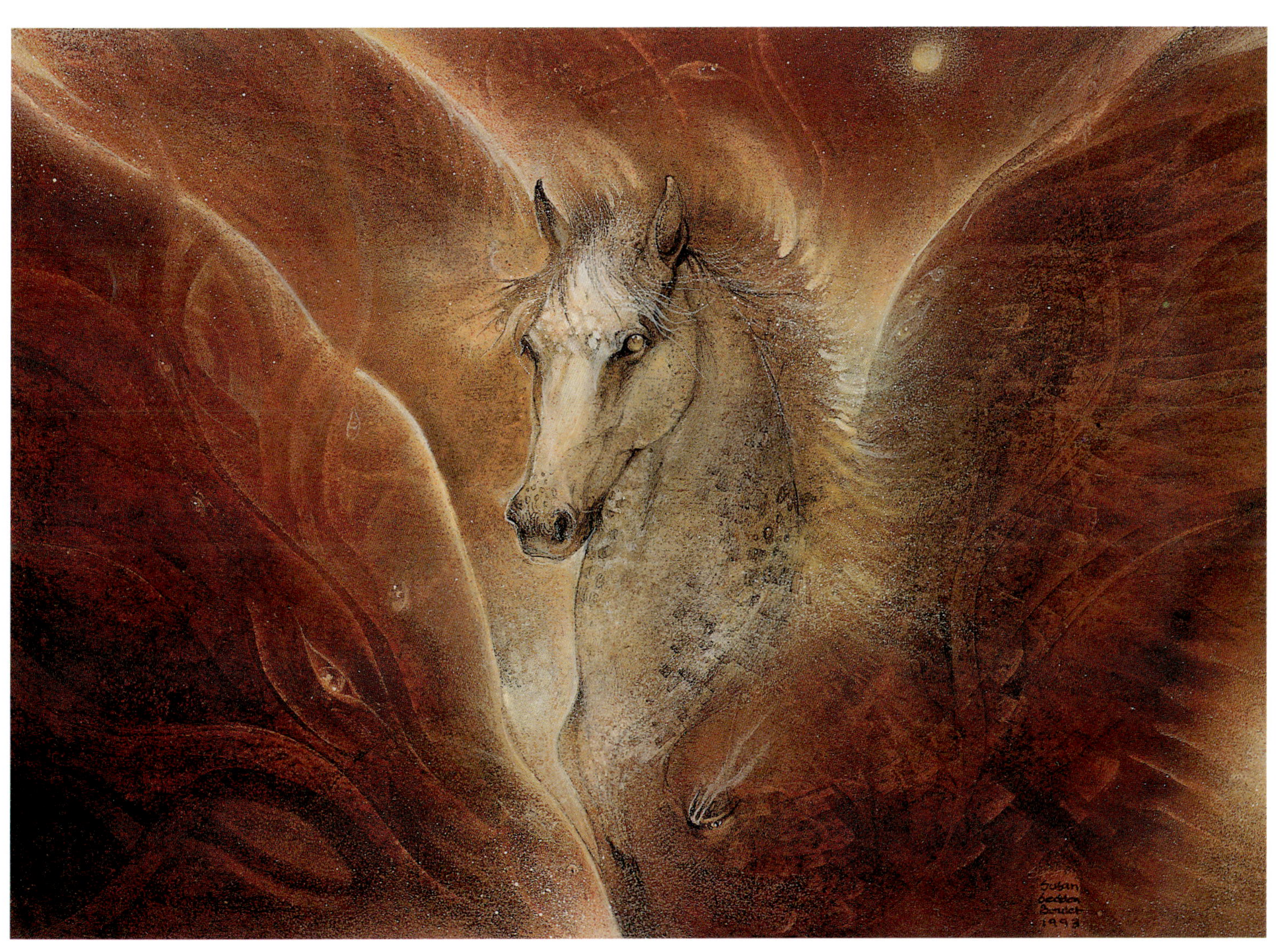
Susan
Seddon
Boulet
1993

Minerva

Although Minerva, the Roman goddess of war and wisdom, is usually portrayed as equivalent to the Greek goddess Athena, she was originally an Etruscan goddess of dawn. She is revered as a goddess of wisdom, for the light of dawn typifies knowledge. She guides heroes in war and is patroness of all arts, crafts, guilds and medicine. Called by Ovid "the goddess of a thousand works," she was the inventor of musical instruments, numbers and many crafts, including weaving. The serpent and the owl were sacred to her. The serpent is an emblem of life energy and the creative impulse. The owl is a symbol of death and wisdom, and thus Minerva, a goddess of the dawn and of wisdom, is also a goddess of death and transformation. Minerva is an incarnation of wisdom in human form, an affirmation that we can use our knowledge and wisdom in the pursuit of any goal we choose.

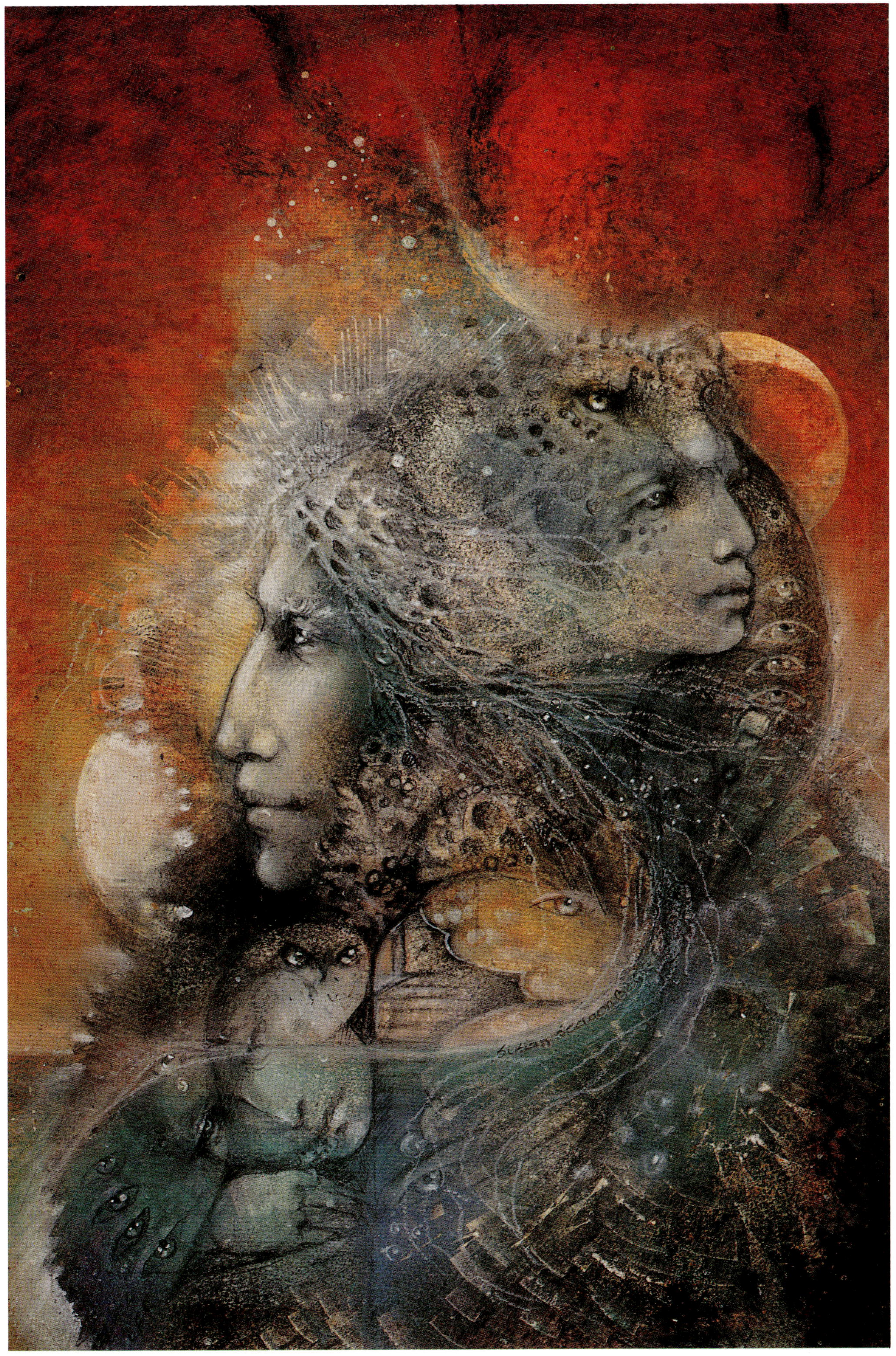

Morgan le Fay

Morgan le Fay is commonly remembered as the enchantress half sister of King Arthur. She is, in fact, the great queen goddess, ruler of the mystical island of Avalon, the Fortunate Island of the Blessed Dead. Sometimes equated with the ancient Irish warrior goddess Morrigan, she is the Celtic death goddess. As Morgana Fata she is the controller of destinies and knows the fate of each person. She is noted for her healing powers, her knowledge of healing plants and her prophetic vision. Like a shaman she is a shape shifter, able to take on many forms. Morgan le Fay represents that deep place of healing magic within each of us—the center where wisdom and healing flow even in the moment of death. The ambivalence with which she is traditionally represented echoes our own fear of her deep and ancient wisdom.

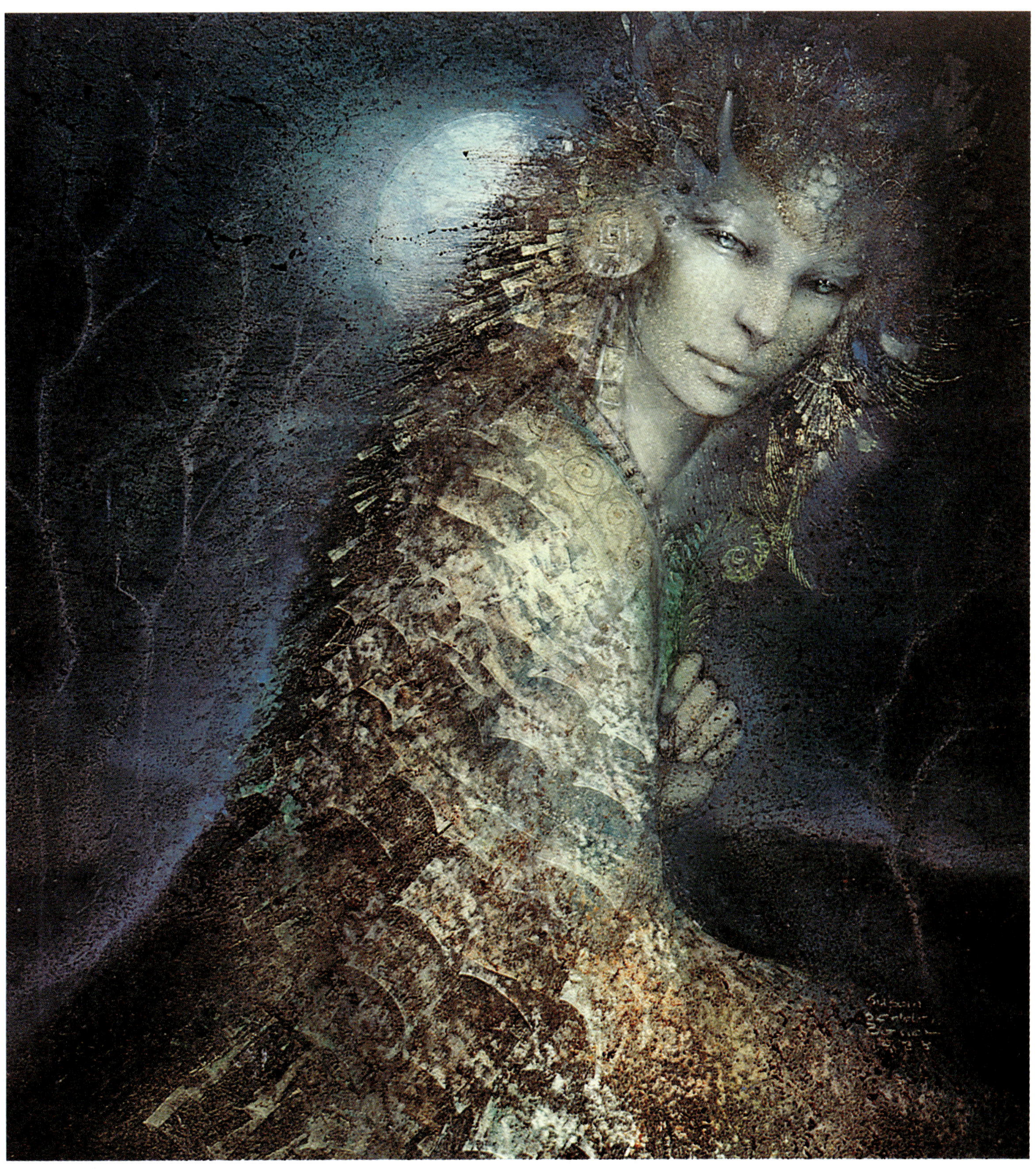

Pele

Pele is the fiery Hawaiian volcano goddess. The daughter of the earth goddess Haimea, Pele came to Hawaii on a boat. Killed in a fight with her sister, the ocean, she took refuge in the glowing cauldron of Mount Kilauea, where she receives the souls of the dead and regenerates them with fire. In a tempestuous relation with Kamapua'a, the ferocious pig god, she is portrayed as a jealous goddess, her jealous rages manifesting as volcanic eruptions. Revered by Hawaiians even today, she carries the force of the volcano, with its molten lava flow, which even in destruction creates new land. Pele stands for the molten, fierce aspect of life that is unable to do anything halfway. She reminds us that even in the midst of fiery eruption there is creation and new life.

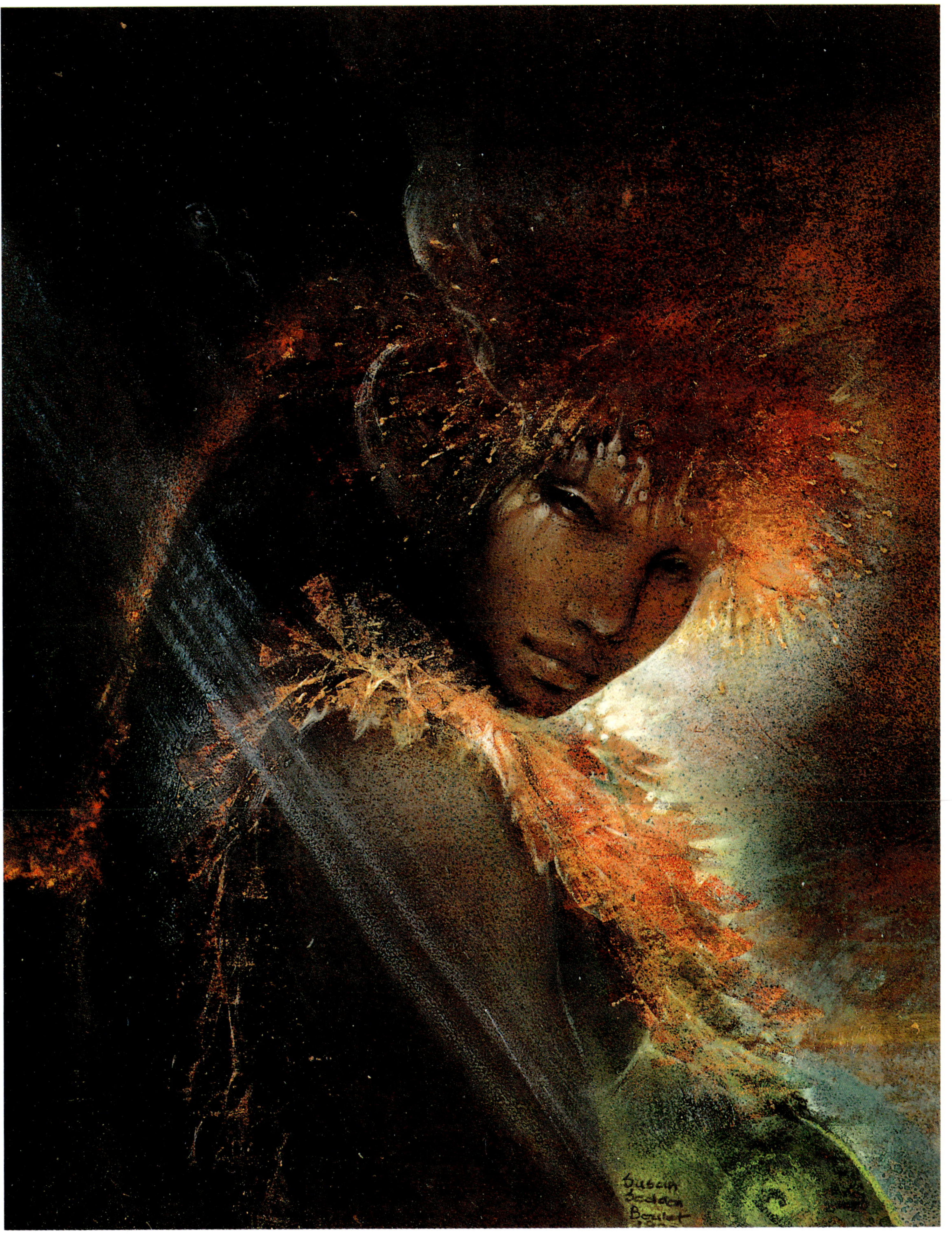
Susan
Seddon
Boulet

Persephone

Although Persephone is best known as Demeter's daughter, the maiden who was abducted by Hades, lord of the underworld, the Greek version of her myth reflects the usurpation of female mysteries by a patriarchal mythology. In this version Persephone personifies the *kore*, the maiden aspect of the goddess. Her myth exemplifies the cycles of nature, for when Persephone is underground plants do not bloom, and when she returns to earth spring ensues.

There is an older version of Persephone: the triple-faced Great Goddess, dark queen of the underworld, creator and destroyer of all life and energy. Her name means "she who brings destruction," indicating her role in the endless cycle of creation, death and rebirth. Persephone is a goddess of the soul, for it is in the darkness of the underworld (analogous to the unconscious) that soul is formed. In the Orphic mysteries, Persephone granted wisdom to the initiate, for she is the goddess of a dark, uncomfortable wisdom; one of her titles is "the saving goddess." Nowhere in mythology does anyone travel to the underworld and find her absent. Persephone is a goddess of dark and frightening power, representing the ability to rule over the aspects of ourselves that are terrifying in the extreme.

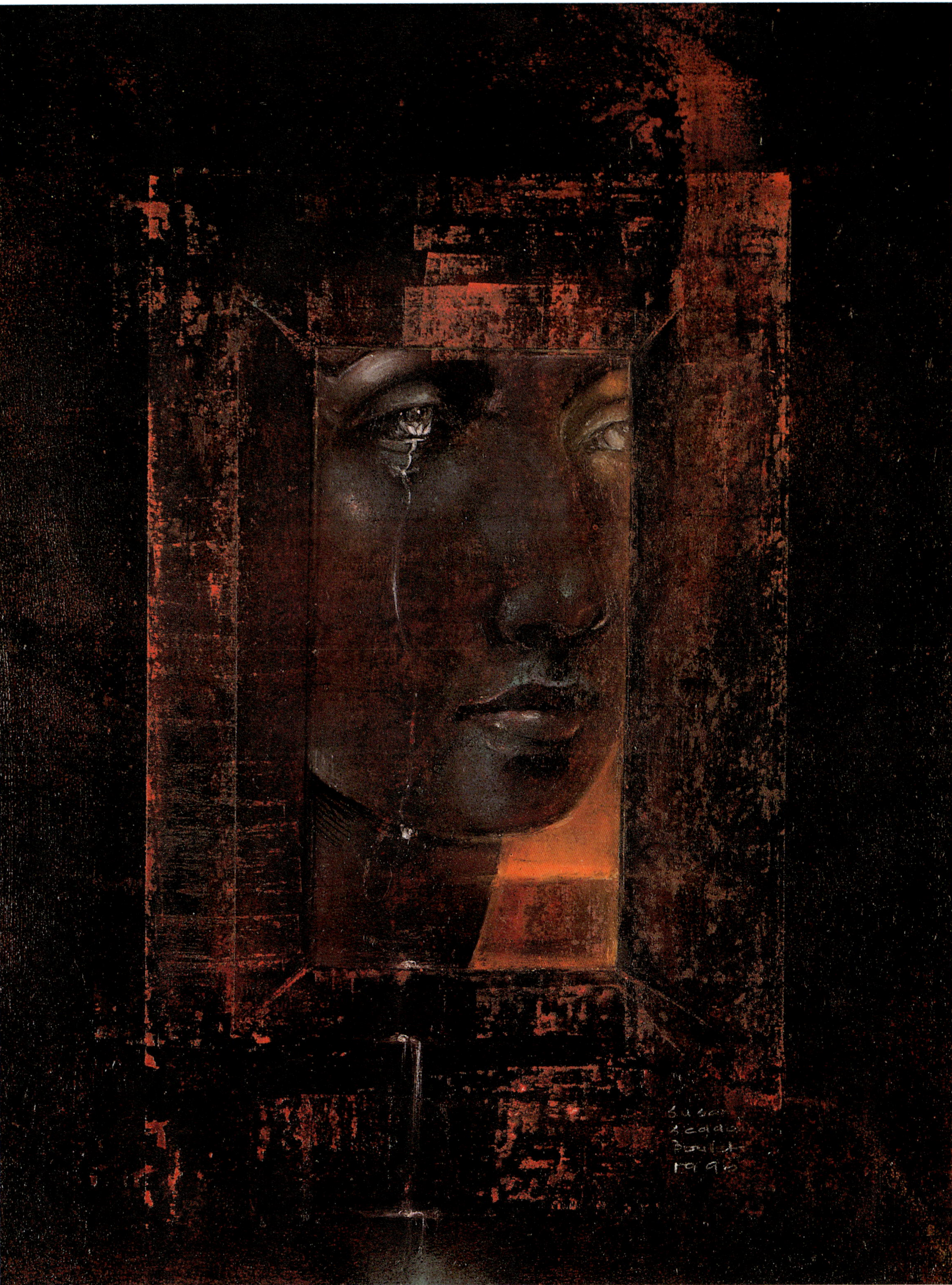

Psyche

The story of Psyche is a story of growth and integration. It tells of a mortal woman taken to a mysterious castle to be married to a fierce dragon. Her husband comes to her in the middle of the night, and she falls in love with him. Told that she must never look upon his face, she disobeys this injunction and finds that her husband is really Eros, the god of love; when he awakes, he flies away, leaving her forever.

Grief-stricken, Psyche roams far and wide trying to find Eros. She goes to his mother, Aphrodite, who gives her four tasks to complete, each seemingly impossible. First, she must sort a roomful of seeds; then she must obtain some golden fleece from a number of fierce rams; her third task is to fill a glass bottle from the waters of the river Styx; and her final task is to descend into Hades and retrieve a box of beauty.

Through the process of meeting the challenges of her tasks and integrating her experiences she grows from an innocent young girl capable only of romantic love into a mature goddess able to love not only herself but also Eros, the god of love. Psyche is a rich reminder of our imperative to grow; she reminds us that the process of life takes us into dark places as well as light, just as the butterfly emerges from the chrysalis.

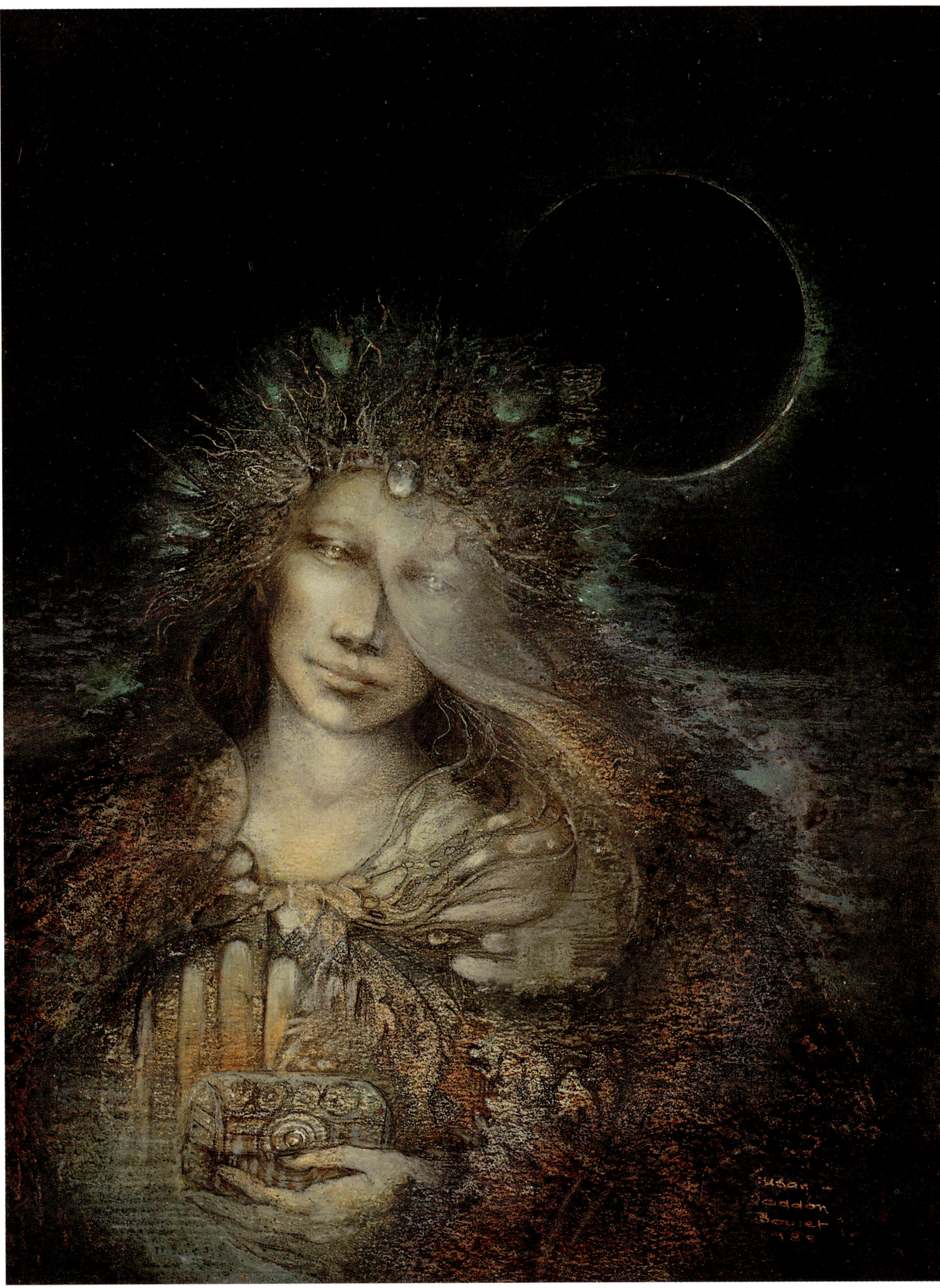
Boulet

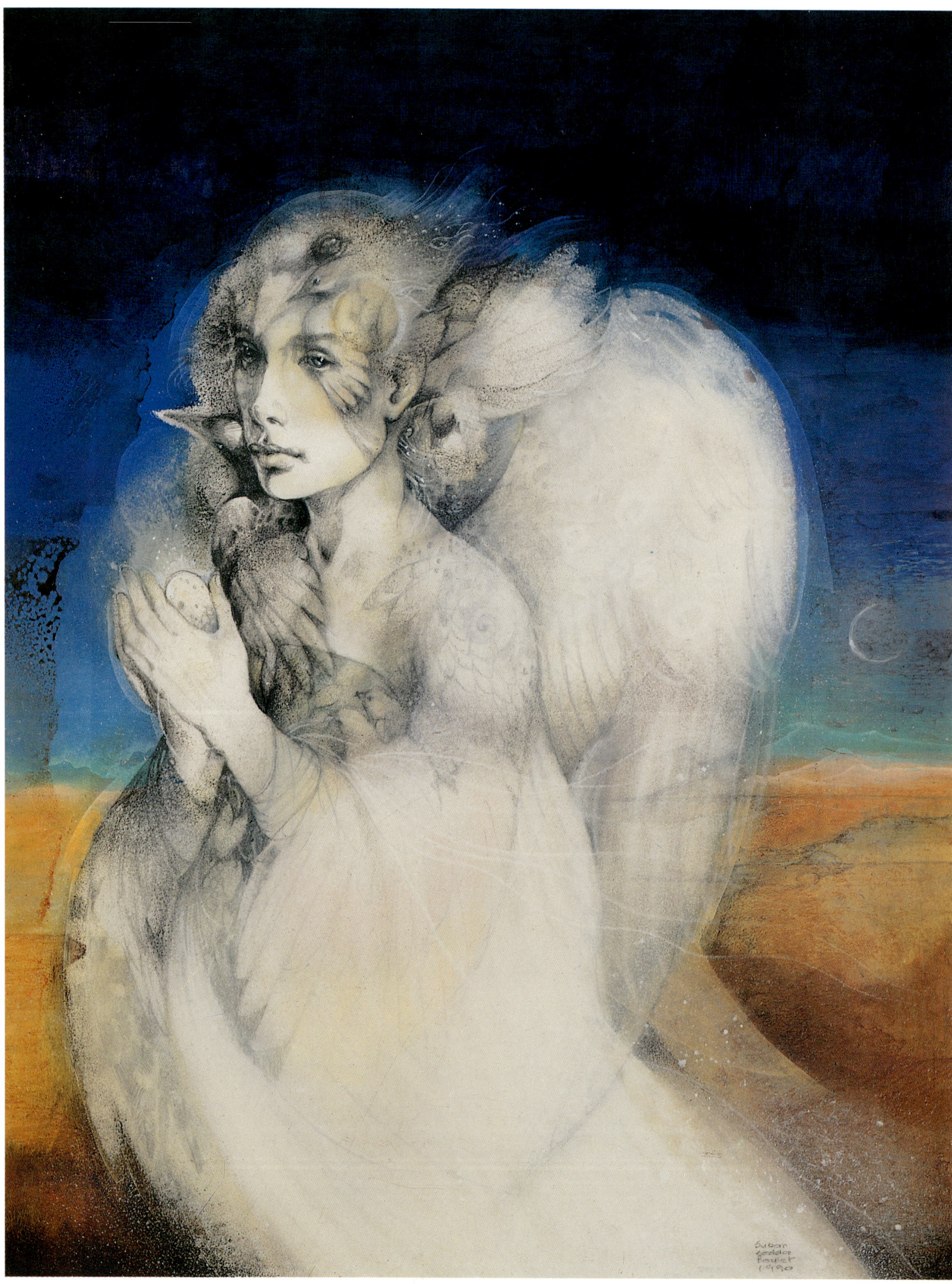
Susan
Seddon
Boulet
1990

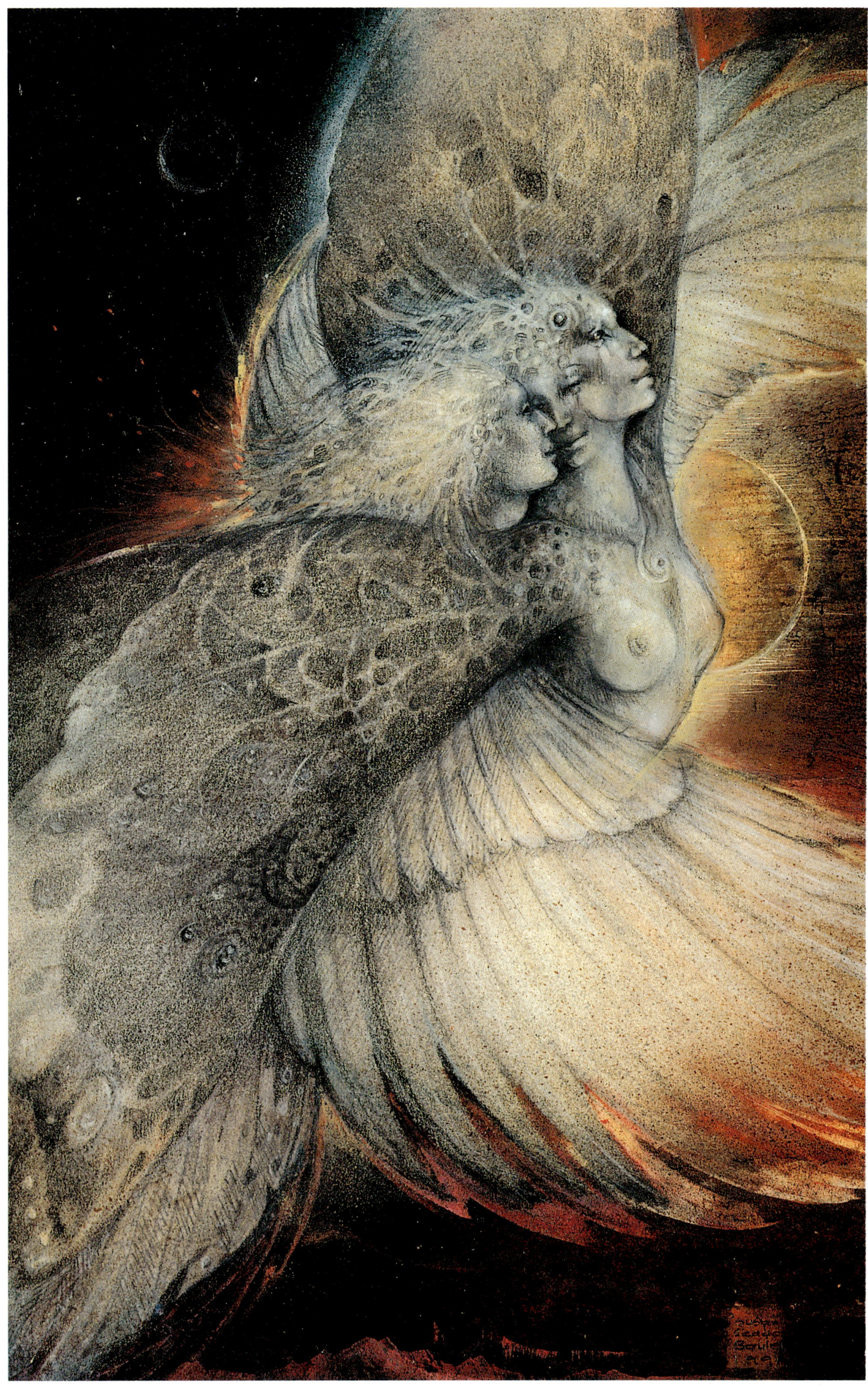

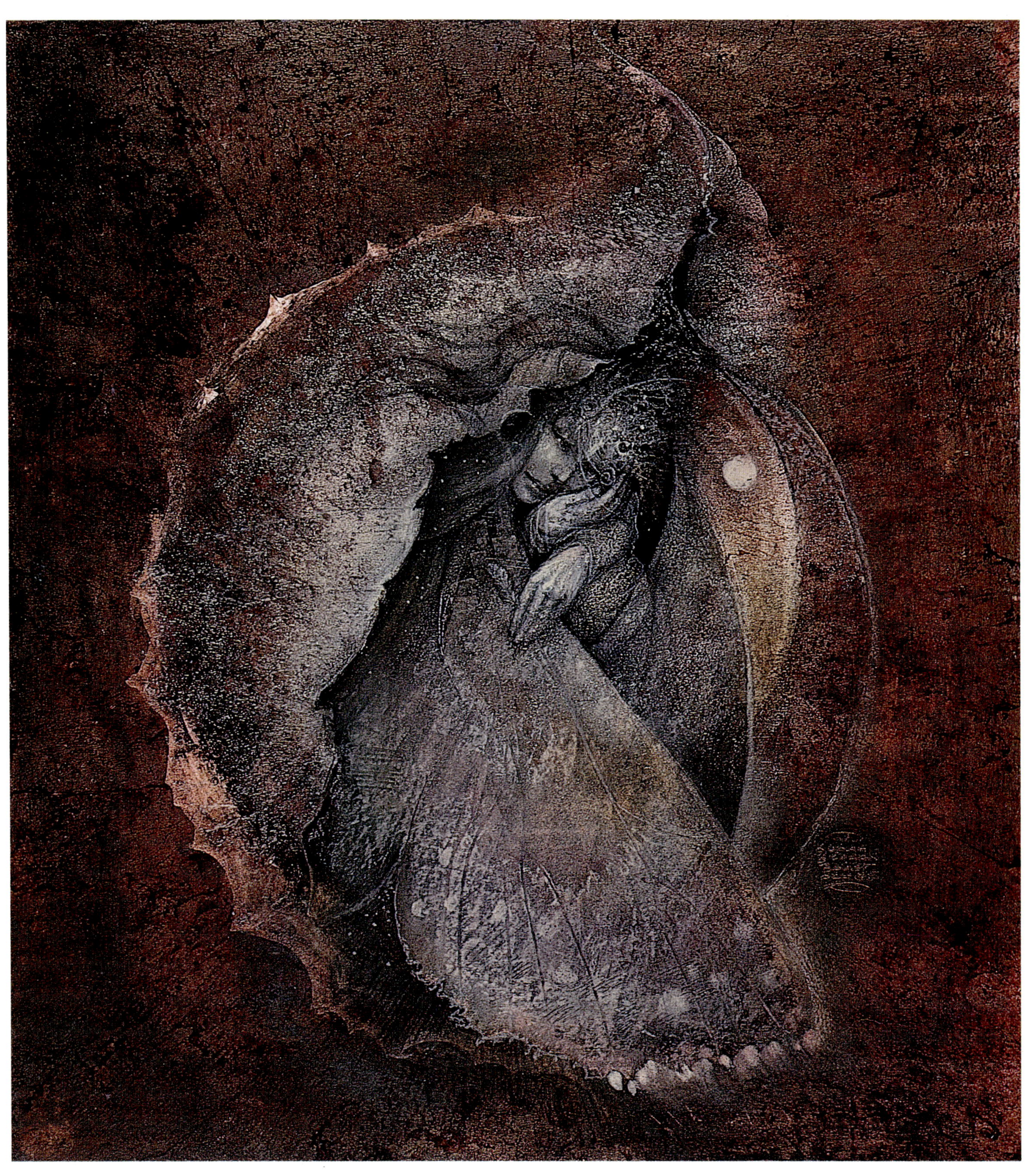

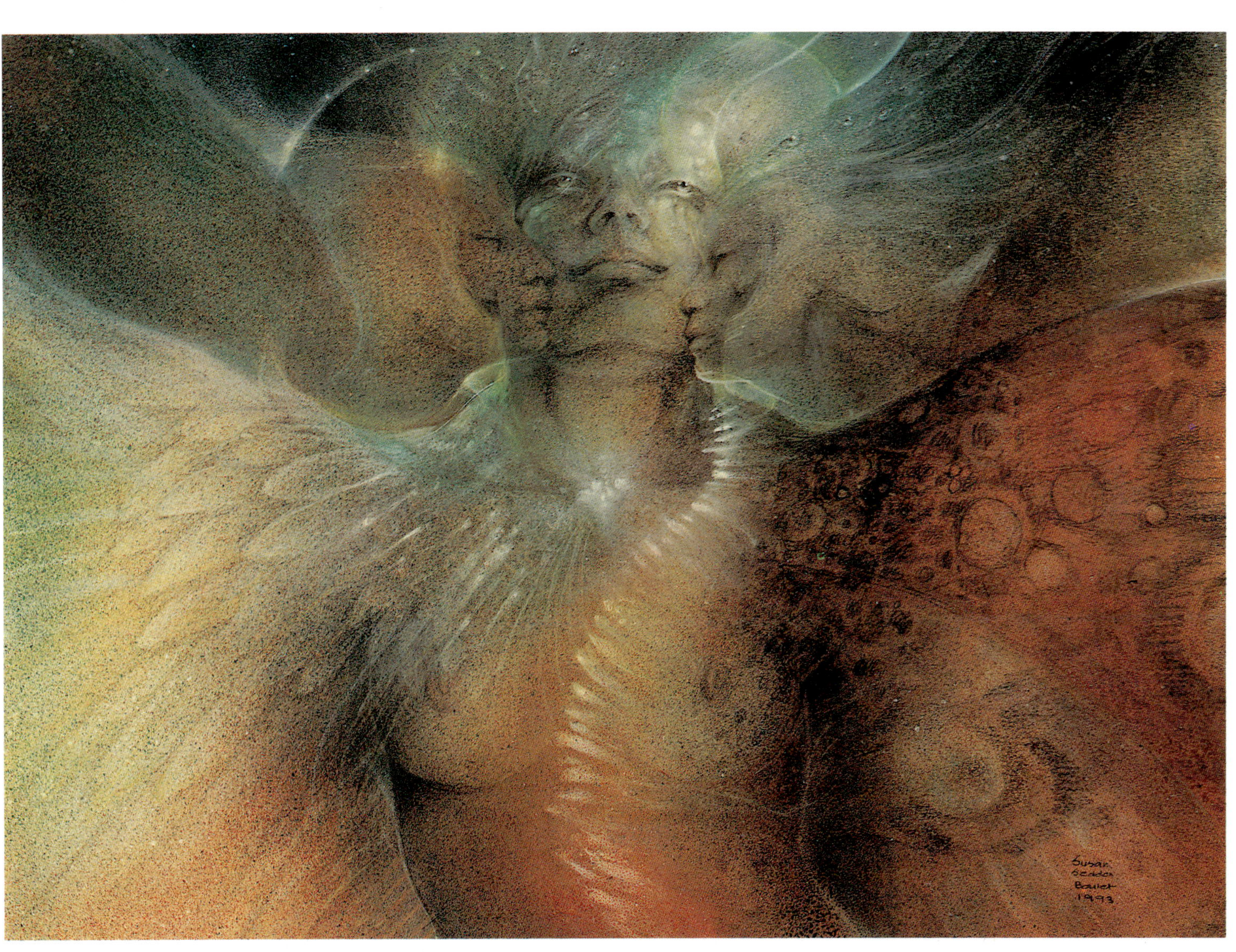
Susan
Seddon
Boulet
1993

Rhiannon

Rhiannon is the Great Goddess as worshiped by the Welsh. She is an embodiment of life, death and rebirth, for in her realm there is no death without regeneration. Her name derives from *Rigantona*, which means "great queen." A shape shifter, she can assume any form she wants; she often appears as a white horse. She is a muse goddess and is accompanied by three sweetly singing birds who can revive the dead or put the living to sleep. The source of the king's power derived from Rhiannon, the queen, and a candidate for kinghood met Rhiannon dressed as a stag, a regal figure symbolic of rejuvenation, beauty, strength and instinctual masculine energy. In later myth she appears as Nimuë or as Vivien, the Lady of the Lake. Rhiannon is a beautiful queen of the night, a reminder of the close balance between death and rebirth. She demands that we honor our instinctual and animal selves as a source of creativity, abundance and order.

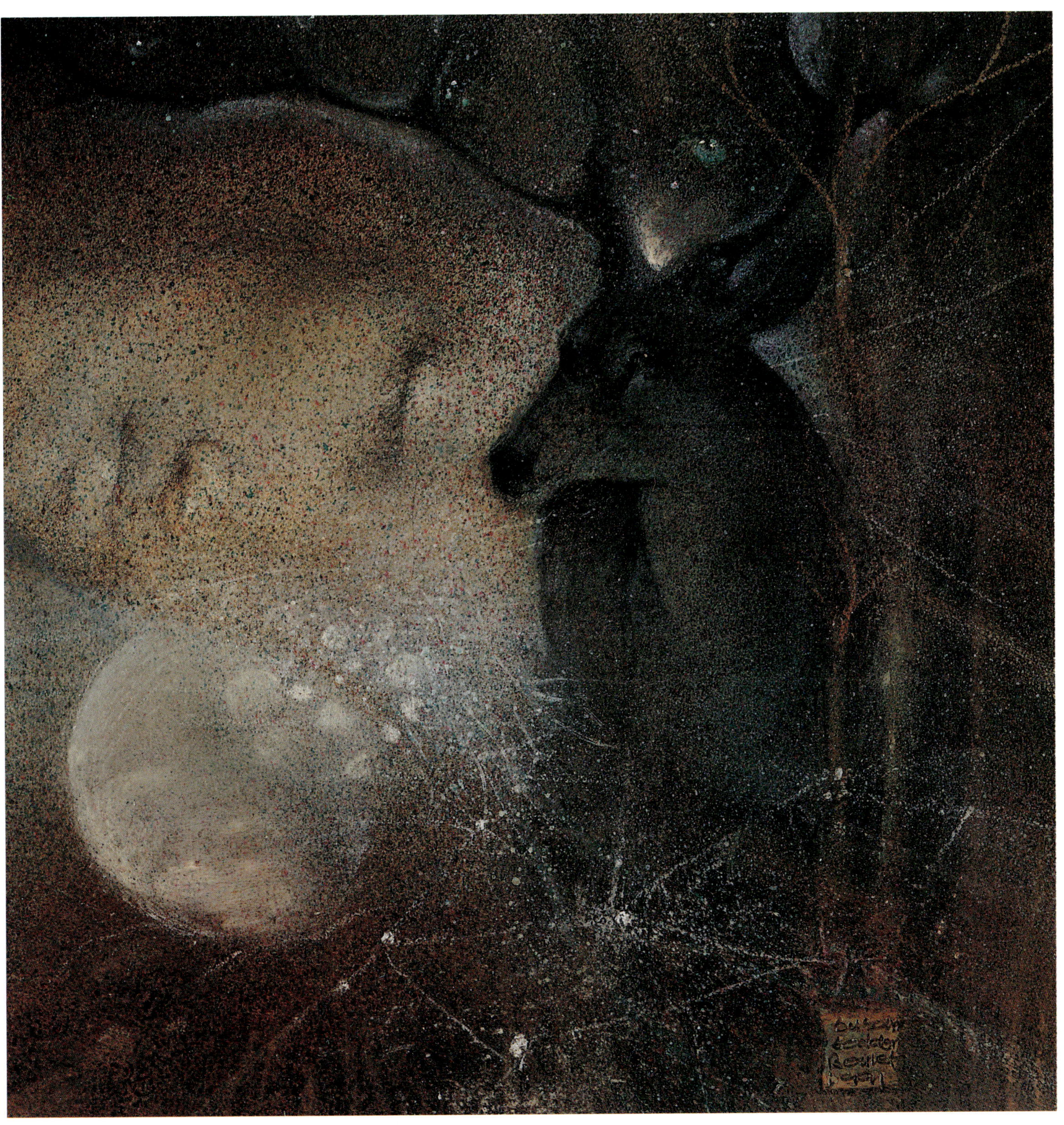

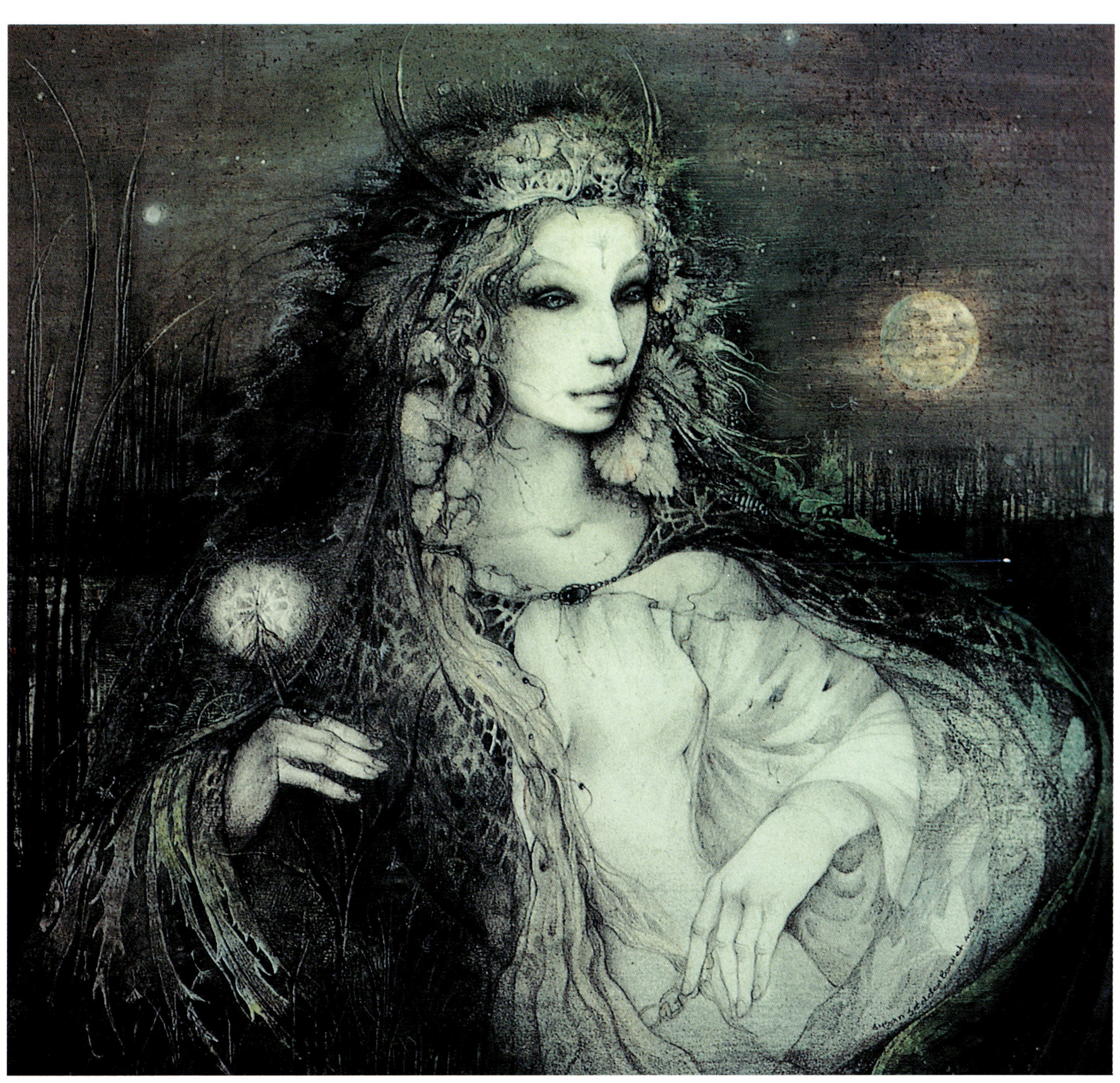

Sedna

Sedna, the source of all nourishment, is one of the best-known figures in central Eskimo mythology. As a young woman Sedna married a man-seabird, who mistreated her. When her father came to take her home, the husband raised a threatening storm. To save his own life, Sedna's father threw her overboard. When she tried to reenter the boat, he used his axe to chop off her fingers, which transformed into seals, whales and all the creatures of the sea. Sedna sank to the bottom of the sea, where she serves as ruler of the souls of the dead. In times of need she is summoned from the sea by an *angakok* (shaman), who plaits and combs her hair. In return, she sends seals and whales to feed the people. Sedna represents the creative force of the sea and the sea's nourishing gifts. When portrayed as somewhat frightening she reflects our fear of the depths she inhabits. She nourishes things seen and unseen.

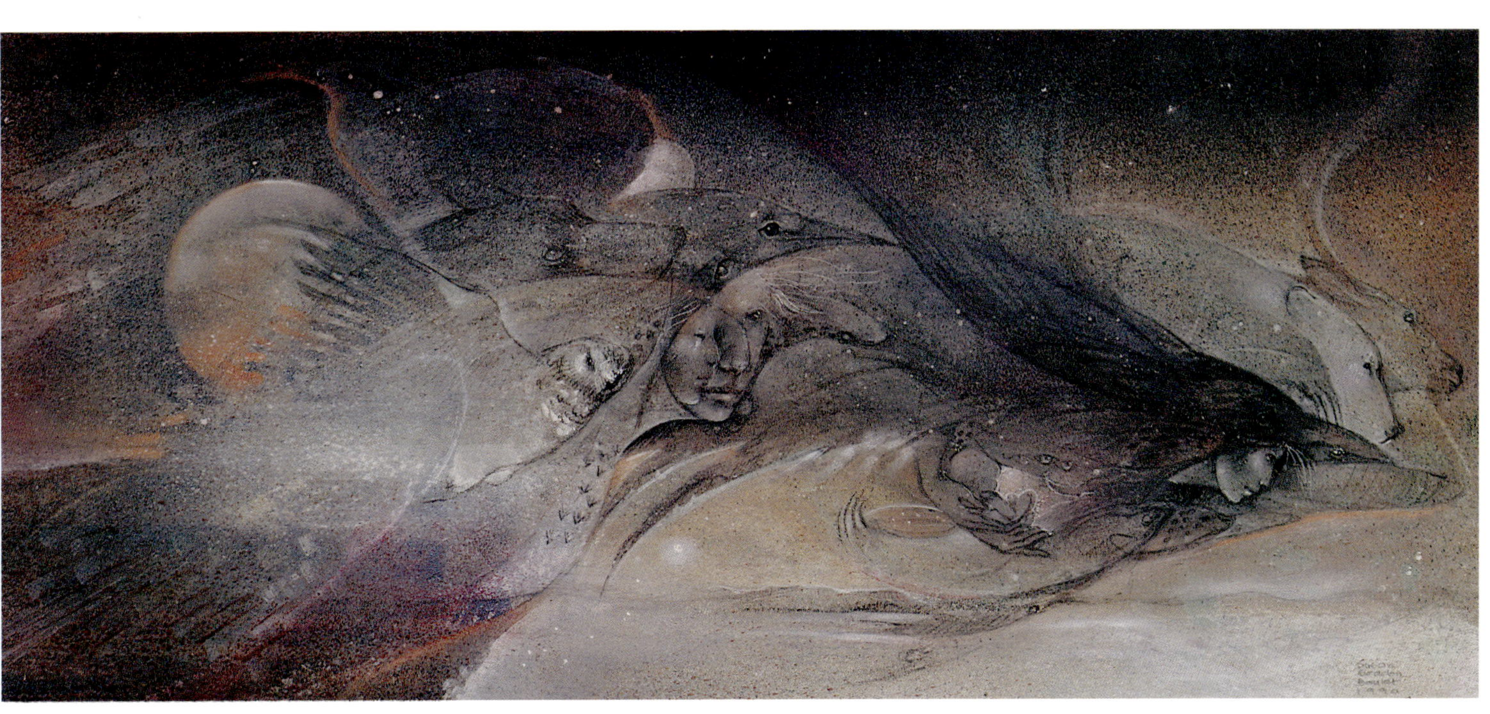

Selene

Selene, Queen of the Starlit Heavens, is the ancient Greek goddess of the moon. She carries the moon across the sky in a white chariot driven by winged horses or bulls. She is the totality of the moon, with its waxing into fullness and waning into darkness. Selene fell in love with a mortal, Endymion. When she descended to the earth to join Endymion, he fell into a deep sleep from which he never awoke. Selene continued to visit him nightly.

In later Greek mythology Selene represented the full moon, while Artemis represented the crescent or waxing moon and Hecate the waning and dark moon; hence Selene is Phoebe, meaning "bright, shining." She is traditionally represented with the crescent moon as a diadem. Selene represents the fullness of life, incorporating all phases of light and darkness in her shining.

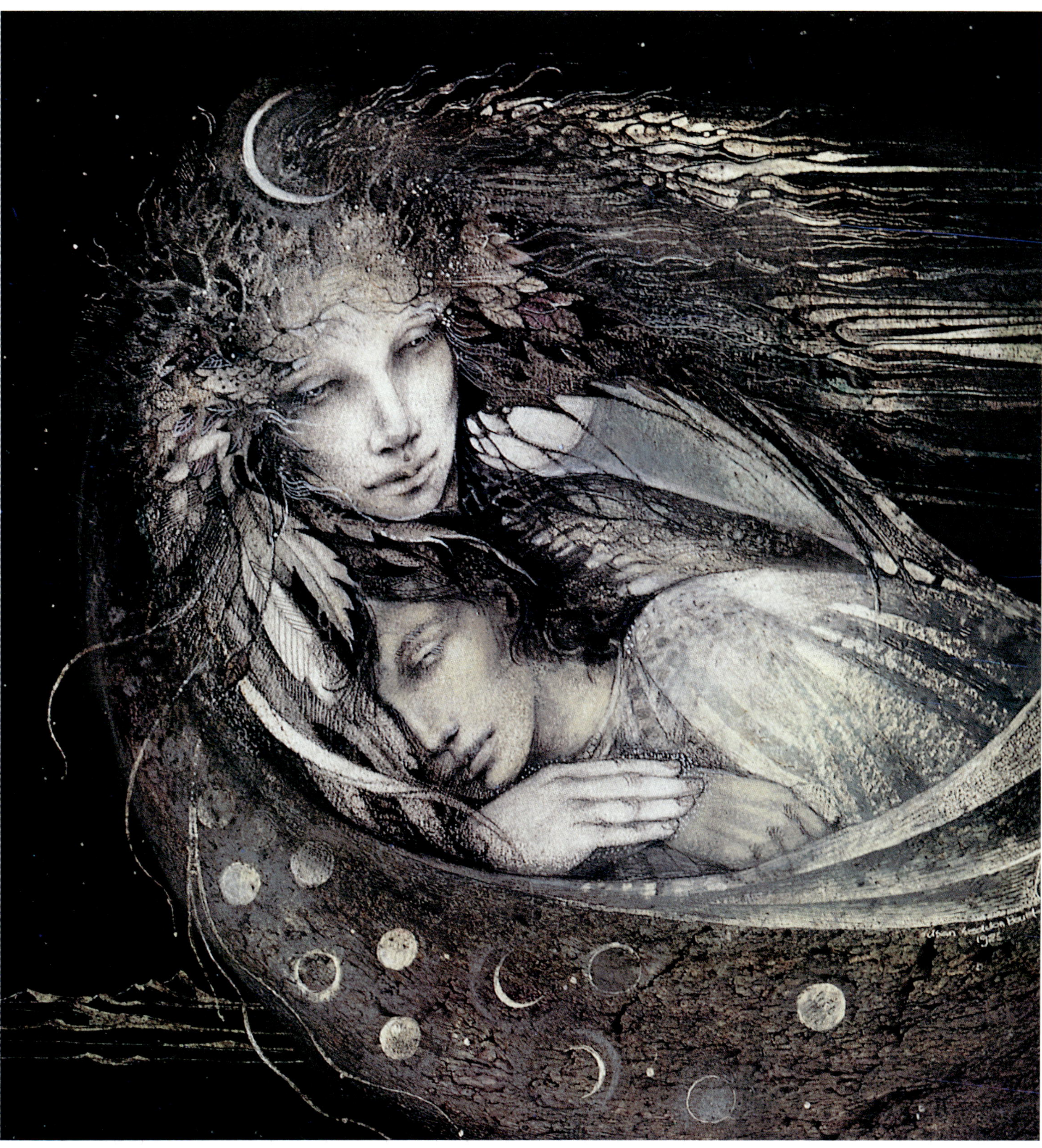

The Sphinx

The Sphinx is an ancient moon goddess, the goddess of birth and death. Part animal, part human, she remains connected to her deep instinctual nature. Most stories emphasize her aspect as death goddess, who carries the dead to the underworld. Often portrayed as a lion, she shares in the solar and regal symbolism of that animal. Her role as an oracular deity, given to enigma and riddles, points to her as a keeper of the great mystery. A symbol of strength, wisdom and royal power, she reminds us that nothing comes to creation without some destruction and that sometimes to solve a mystery we must enter the darkness. This image reminds us that there is beauty even in the heart of that which terrifies.

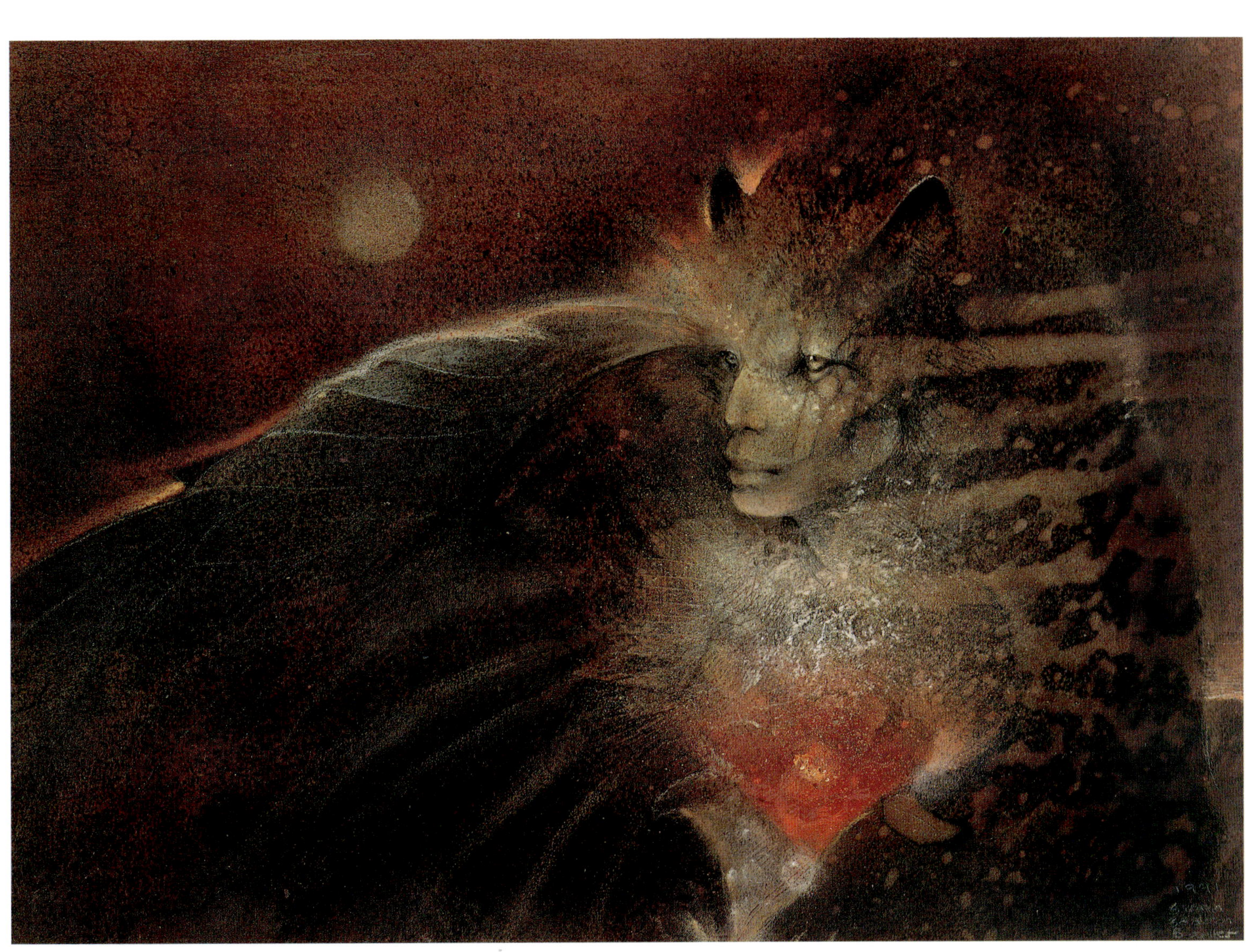

Themis

Themis is one of the oldest and most revered of the Greek goddesses. The daughter of Gaia, the earth goddess, Themis is the mother of the three Fates, who determine the destiny of all mortals and gods. Shown here as the giver of dreams, she once was consulted at Delphi as the bestower of oracles. Themis is prophecy incarnate: her oracles derive from her sense of order and connection to nature. In later Greek mythology, transferred to Mount Olympus, she personified the social order of law and custom, a reminder that social order is ultimately dependent on the natural order of the earth. Themis is a grounded, earthy goddess who is also comfortable moving through the shifting, mantic world of dreams. She is deep wisdom familiar with both the depths of earth and the heights of sky: a guide into soul.

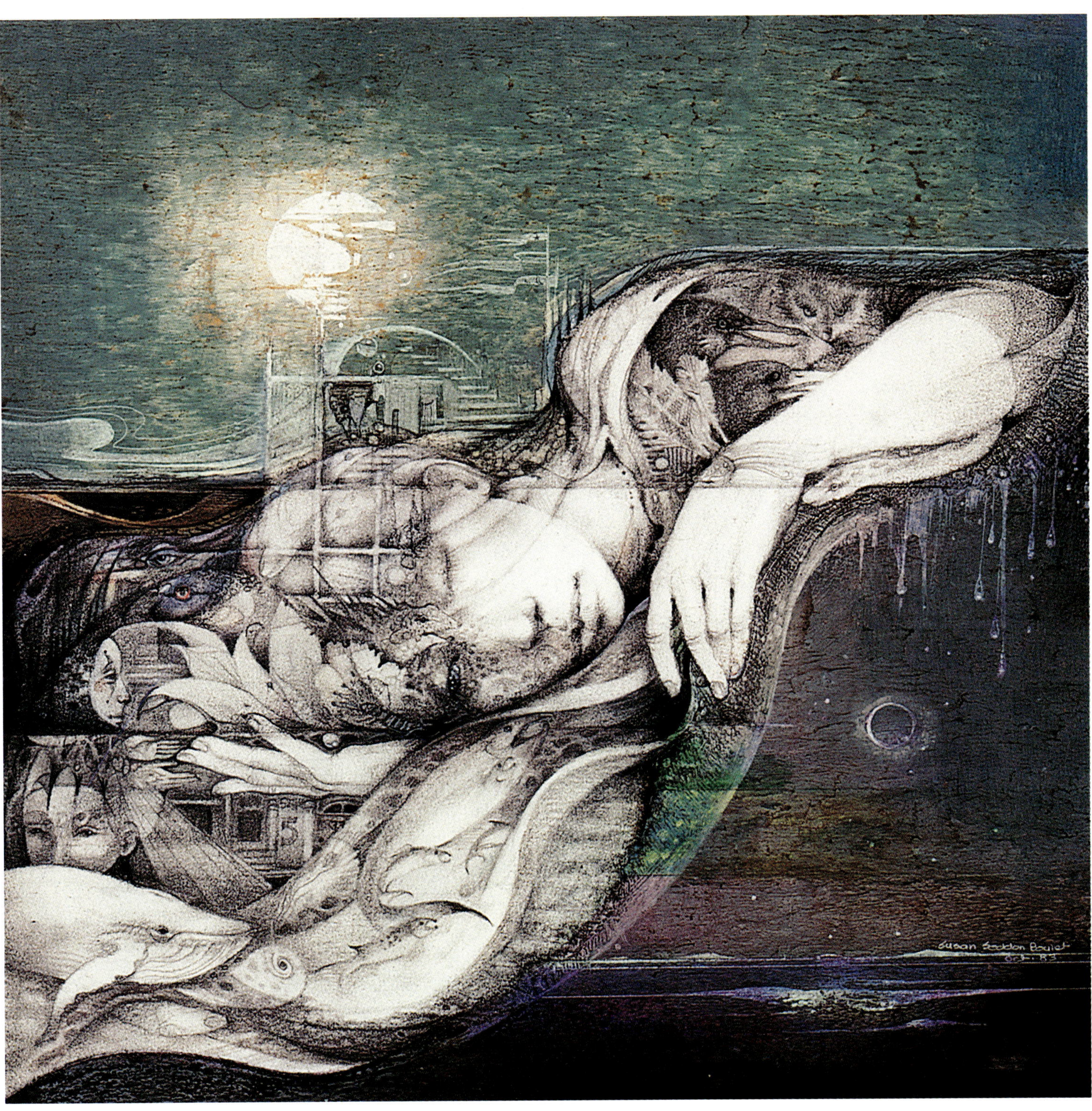
Susan Seddon Boulet

Thetis

Thetis is a Greek sea goddess who represents fertility. She is a creator goddess, for all life begins in the sea, and she is usually portrayed as a Nereid (sea nymph): a beautiful, young semidivine goddess fond of dancing and singing. She helped raise the artisan god Hephaestus and once provided sanctuary for Dionysus. Thetis is particularly known as a shape shifter: when Peleus desired to marry her, she transformed herself into fire, water, a lion and a serpent in order to escape him. As the personification of calm waters, Thetis is responsible for providing a peaceful sea. She is that center of peace and calm that is always available, even in the midst of changing forms. She is a goddess who enjoys life's pleasures.

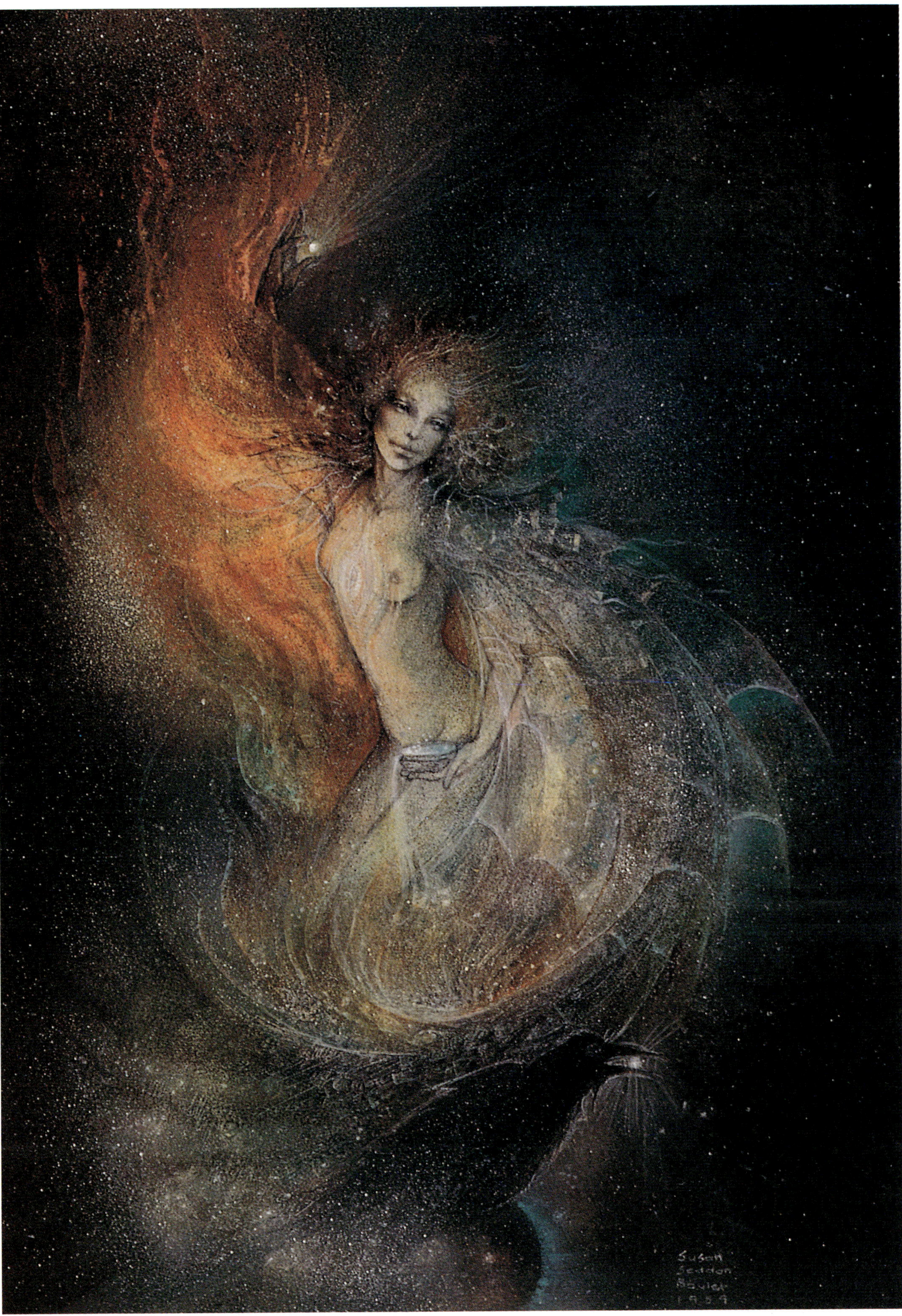
Susan
Seddon
Boulet

Titania and Oberon

Titania and Oberon are best known as the queen and king of the fairies in Shakespeare's *A Midsummer Night's Dream.* Fairies, somewhat evanescent, mostly benign supernatural beings, are probably remnants from an older, goddess-worshiping people; thus Titania and Oberon are ancient Celtic deities. Titania is the Great Mother, an ancient fertility goddess. Her name may refer to her as "mother of the Titans"; hence she is Gaia, the earth goddess. She is also associated with Diana, the moon goddess, mistress of beasts and mother of animals. Oberon is derived from the Teutonic Alberich, king of the underworld and master of all hidden wealth. Titania and Oberon are the mother and father in us all. As queen and king of the fairies they remind us that the depths of earth and underworld also have a light, approachable and playful side.

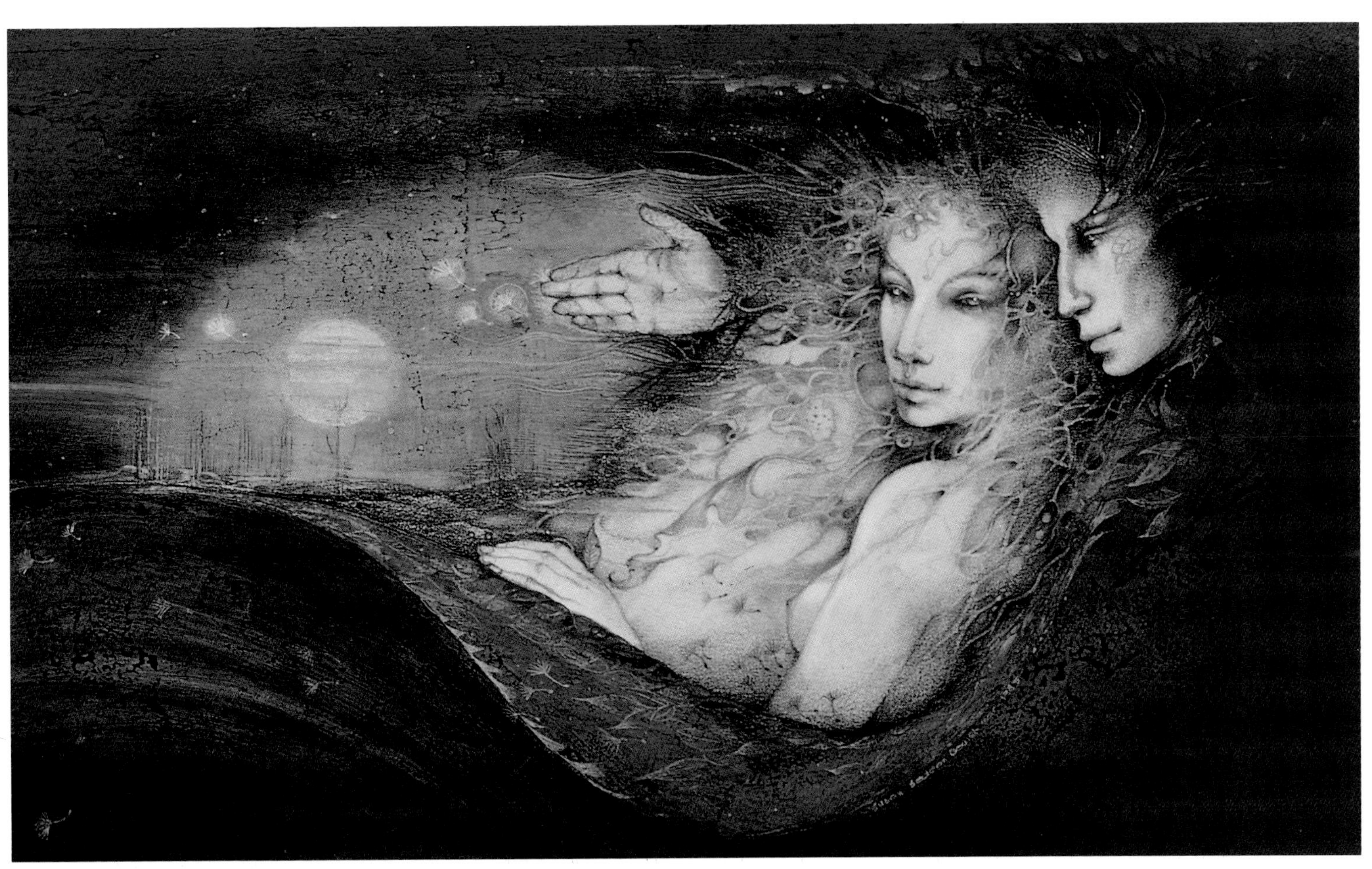

Tlazolteotl

Tlazolteotl is a Toltec earth mother, the goddess of carnal love and desire. Like Kali in India, she is portrayed as a horrible, devouring figure yet is also honored as a moving, creative principle. She is sometimes pictured as four sisters (the four ages of woman), who are present at the crossroads of one's life. Tlazolteotl is best known as the Eater of Impurities. Once in a lifetime, a person confessed her worst deeds and sins to Tlazolteotl, holding back nothing. In return the confessor received absolution: no impurity or defilement was too great to be forgiven. Tlazolteotl is that deep part of ourselves that we fear because it is so powerful and unfamiliar. Yet when we touch her through her fearsome countenance, we find absolute mercy. She is proof that anything that can overwhelm and destroy us also has the power to heal and grant forgiveness.

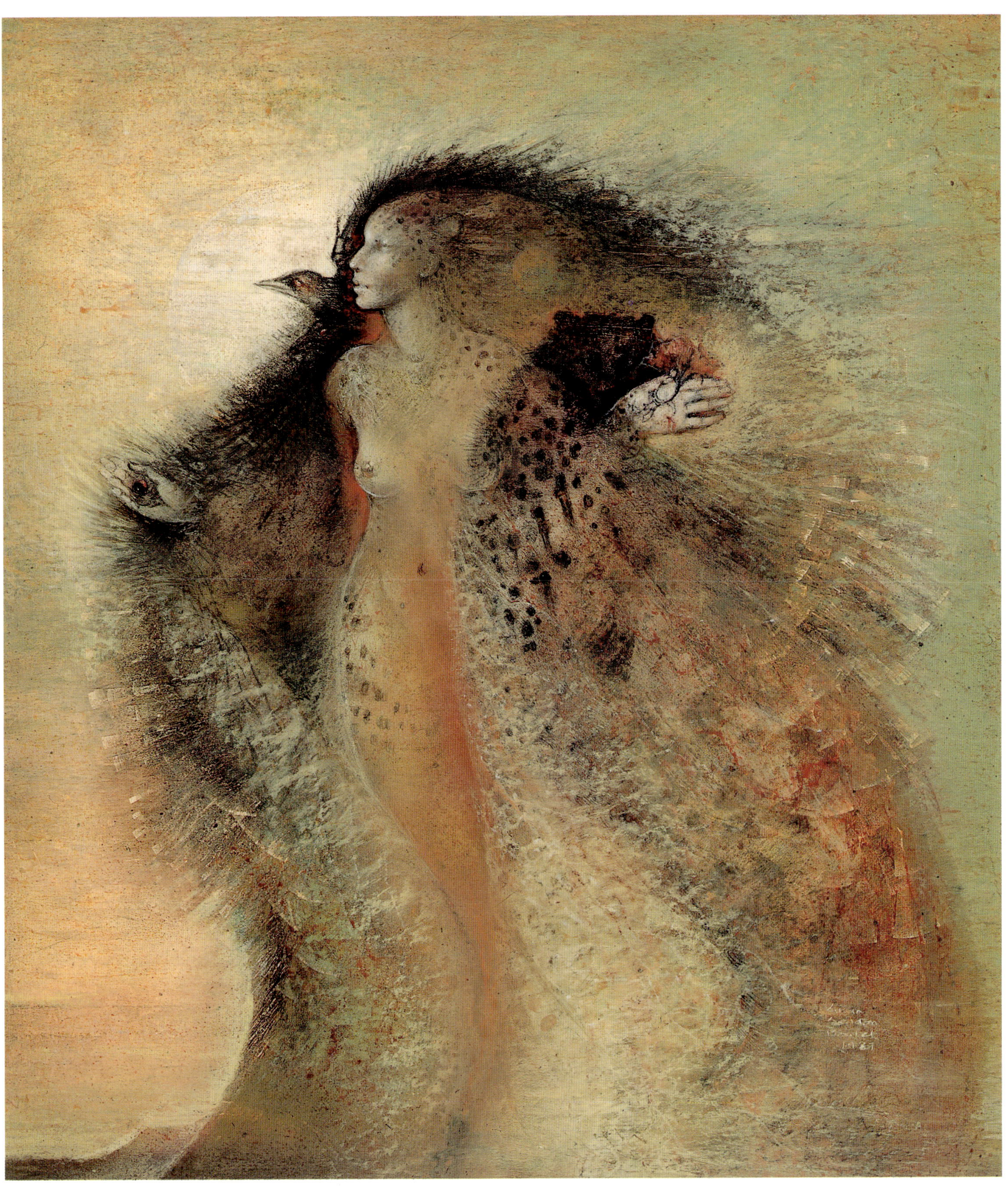

Triple Goddess

The Triple Goddess, the original trinity, symbolizes the three faces of the Great Goddess and is the earliest representation of her division into multiplicity. The goddess with three faces is a universal motif, found worldwide. The Triple Goddess is intimately associated with the changing phases of the moon; just as the moon transforms from one phase to another, the Great Goddess moves among her many roles. Her three faces are usually virgin, mother and crone: virgin representing the strong, self-defined goddess; mother representing the nurturing goddess as source of all nourishment; and crone representing the goddess of death and transformation. This symbolism embraces the role of the goddess in all phases of existence, from birth through death to rebirth. The Triple Goddess reminds us of our sacredness regardless of our age or function in life. It reminds us that despite her many forms there is one goddess, always present and always sacred.

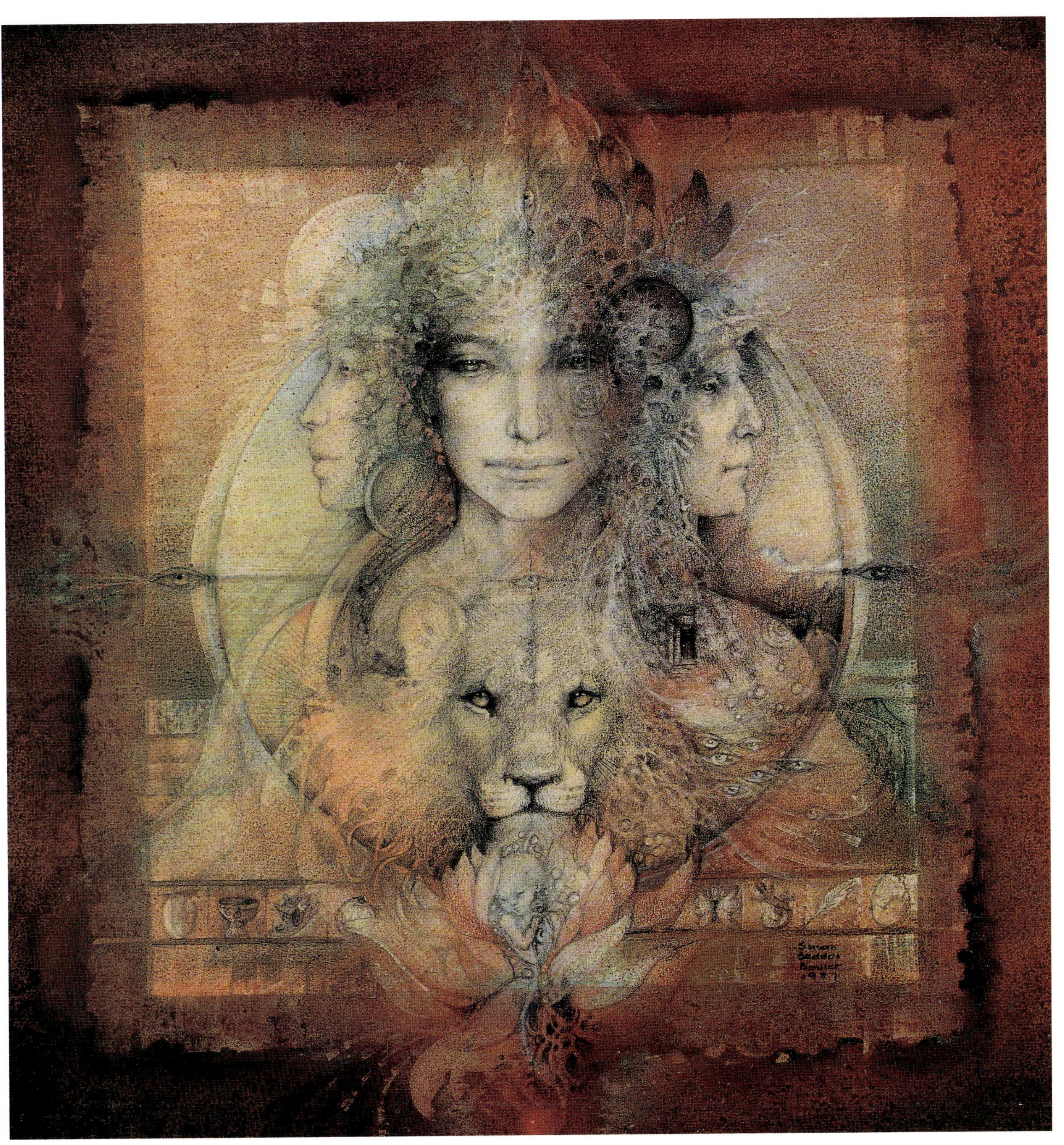

Unelanuhi

Unelanuhi, the Cherokee sun goddess, is one of the few female sun deities found throughout the worldwide pantheon of goddesses and gods. Originally the earth had no sun: it was Spider Woman who pulled Unelanuhi into the sky from the underworld after the other animals had tried and failed. Although she belongs to no one, she and her brother, the moon, are lovers, and they chase each other through the heavens. Her name means "apportioner," for Unelanuhi creates time with her movement through the sky. She is a joyous affirmation of the bright, radiant feminine energy that provides light and warmth to all the world.

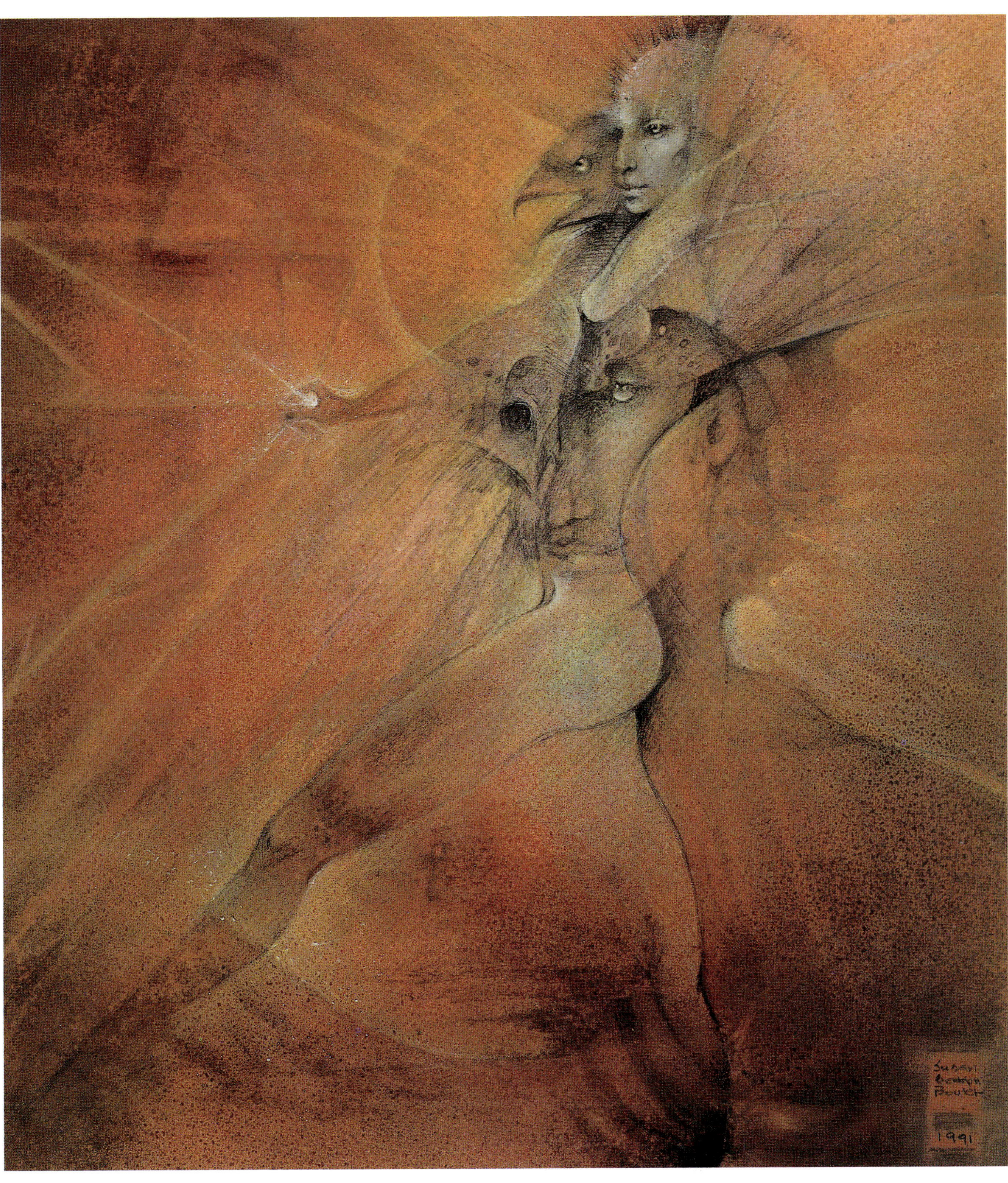
1991

Valkyrie

The goddess appears here as a Valkyrie, a northern European goddess in bird form. There are said to be either nine or thirteen Valkyries. The Bird Goddess is one of the most ancient goddesses, both a parthenogenetic, life-giving creator and a goddess of death and regeneration. The Valkyrie is a representation of this goddess as death wielder.

The bird guise of the Valkyrie is that of the raven, long associated with death and magic. The name Valkyrie means "chooser of the slain"; the face and form of the Valkyrie are the last thing a person sees before death. Valkyries are psychopomps, who lead the soul to the afterworld. For ancient people death was part of a cyclical process leading again to rebirth; black was a positive color, a symbol of fertility and abundance. The Valkyrie represents that part of us that is unafraid of the dark places; she can lead us into and through them. She reminds us that seeds germinate in the darkness, that sometimes we need darkness in order to grow.

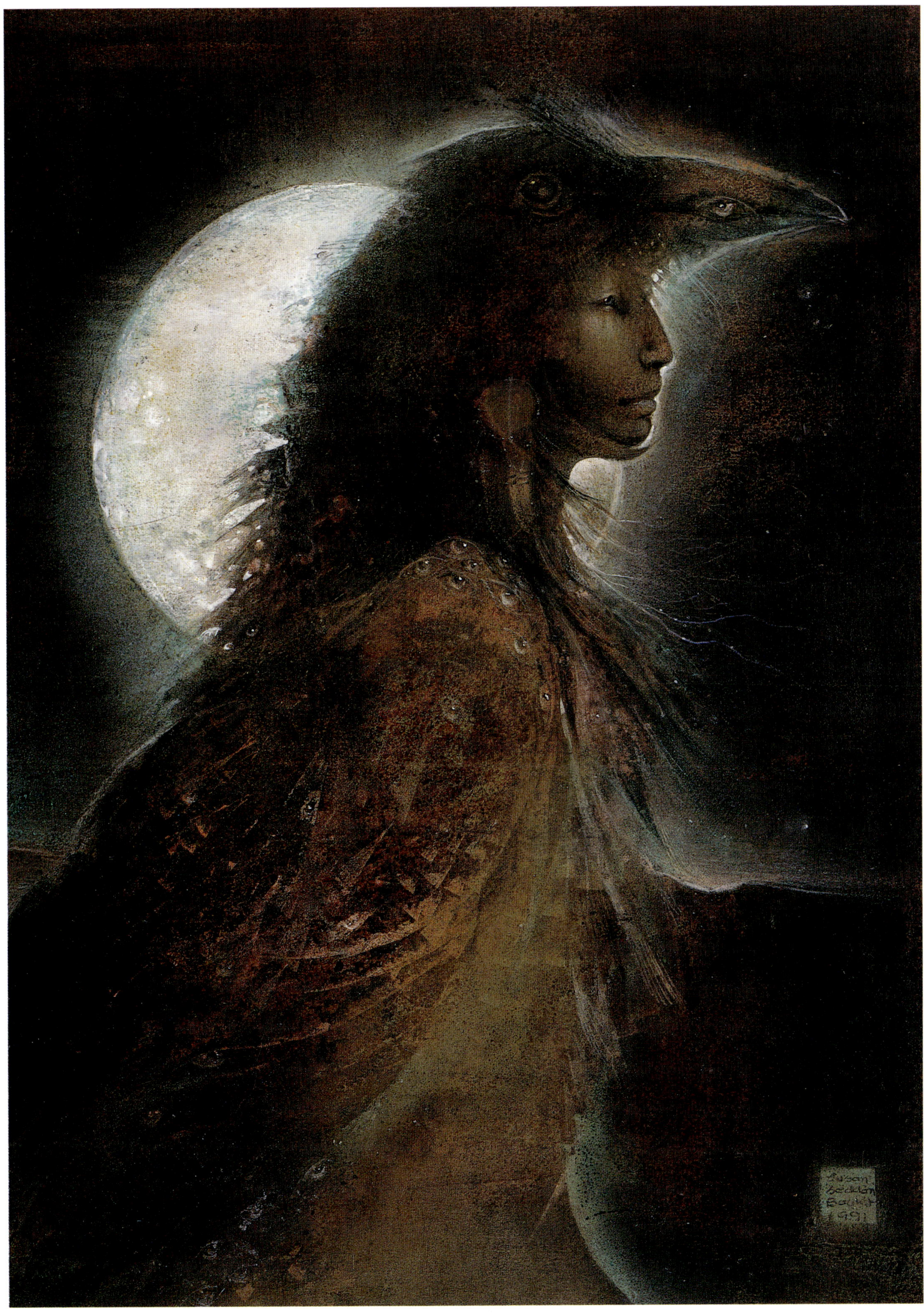

Venus

Venus is the Roman goddess of grace and love, called Aphrodite by the Greeks. She evolved from an early Italian nature goddess, a bringer of spring blooms and vines, a goddess of growth and the beauty of nature. In Latin her name means "to love, desire or charm," and its root provides the words *winsome, wish* and *venerate.* The goddess of desire, Venus was the irresistible personification of both physical and spiritual love. She gave her name to the second planet of dawn and dusk, as did her sister goddesses, Inanna (Sumeria) and Ishtar (Babylonia). Two of her titles were Alma ("nourishing, kind") and Placidus ("quiet, still, gentle").

The story of Venus's birth tells how she arose, naked, from the sea, the source of all life (primordial creation) and a symbol of both the collective unconscious and eternity. It is a wonderful image for the emergence of a young woman into her full femininity. Venus is a striking affirmation of the love of beauty and the pleasure of the senses. Risen from the sea, she is a guide through both the stormy and calm waters of our physical desires and emotions.

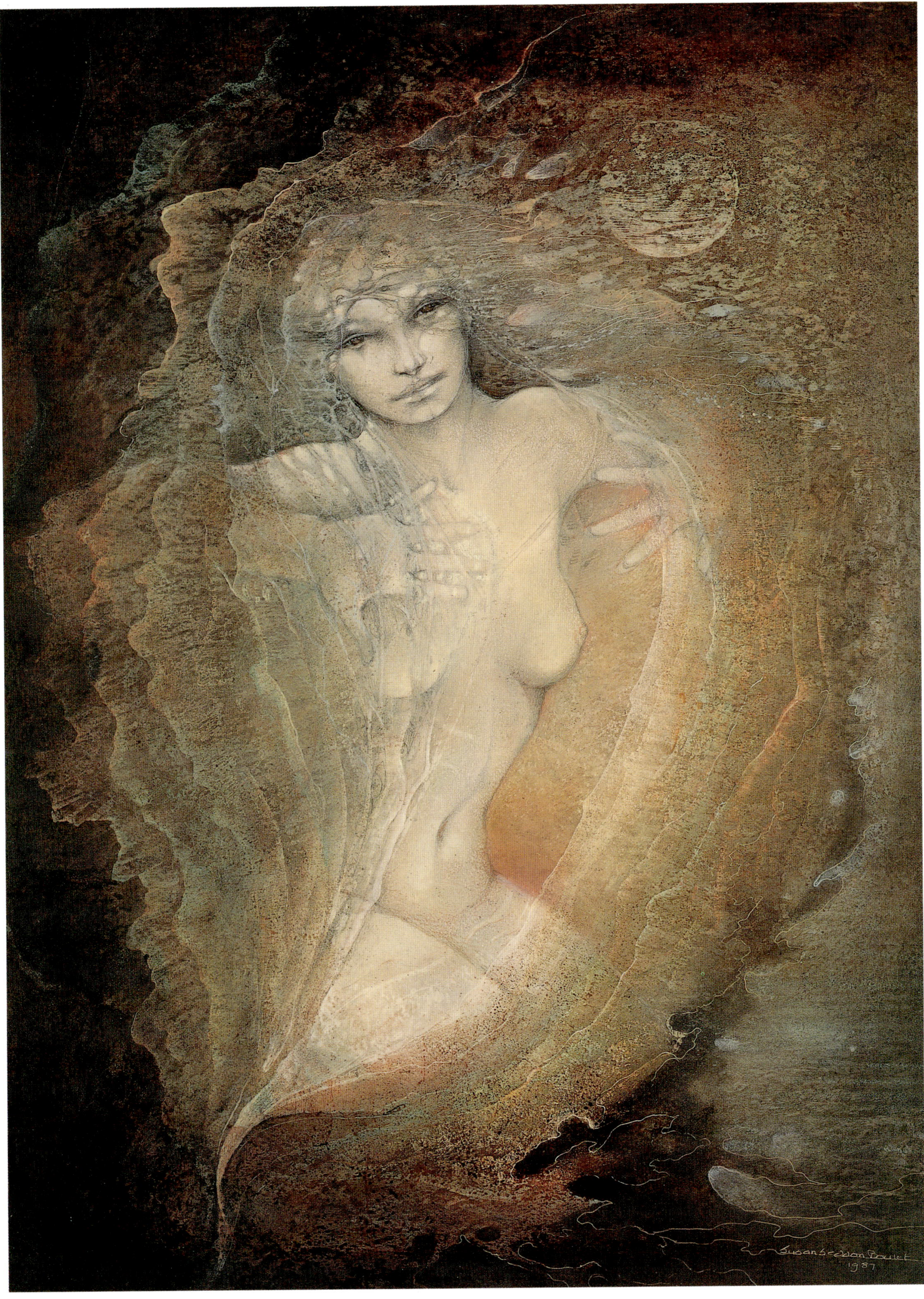

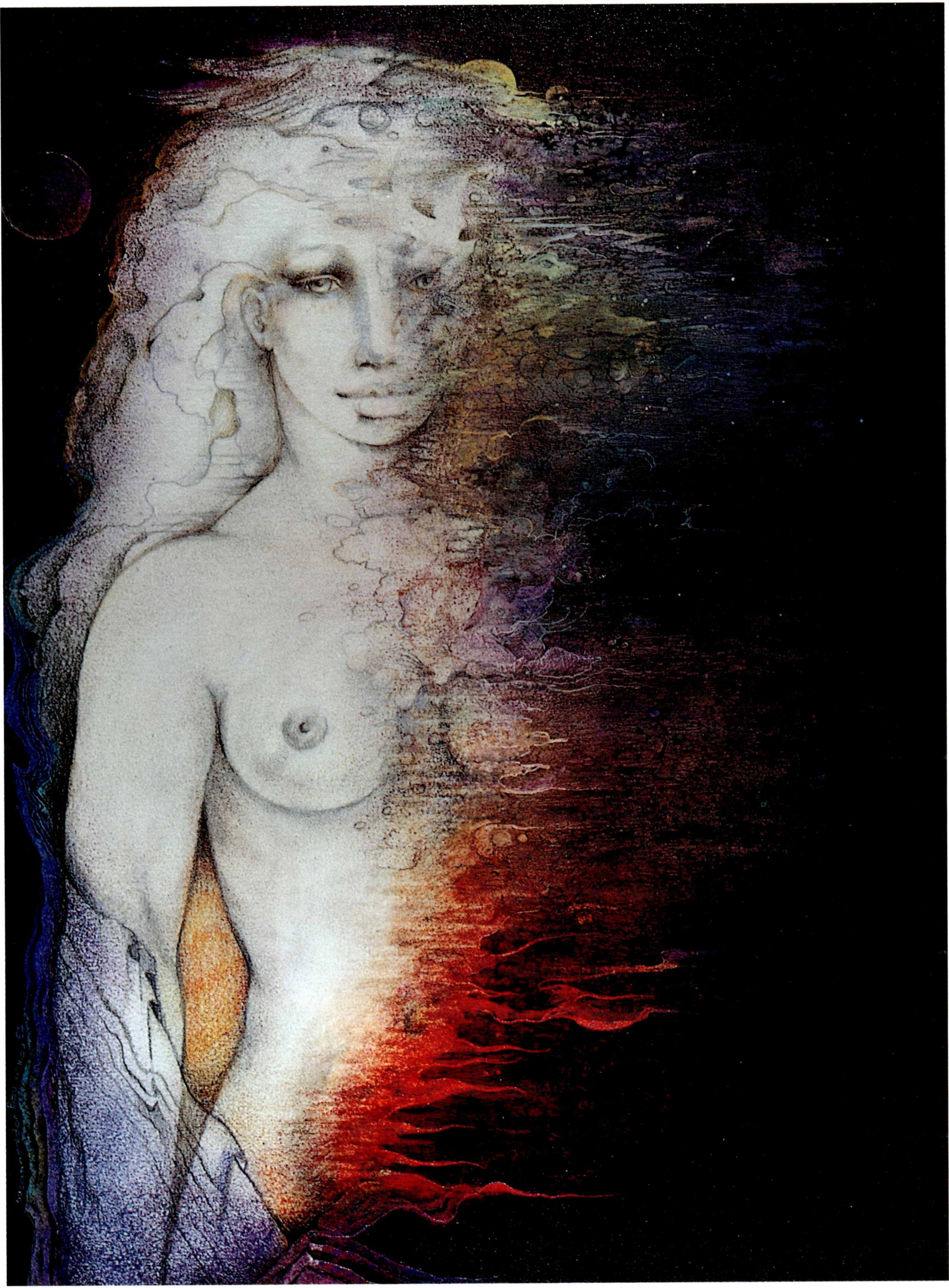

White Shell Woman

White Shell (or White Bead) Woman, also called Turquoise Woman and Abalone Woman, is sometimes said to be a younger version of Changing Woman. White is the color of dawn and of the east. White Shell Woman, the creator and sustainer of life, created the Navajo people and sent them to their home. As gifts, she gave them shells, which became corn and other food-bearing plants; she gave them the animals; she gave them the gifts of rain and beautiful flowers. With the sun, she is the mother of Killer-of-Enemies and Child-of-the-Water, the dual protectors of the people from their enemies.

A Navajo chant says: "All things around me are restored in beauty." It is because of White Shell Woman that this is so, and it is because of her teachings that we can experience the exquisite harmony that comes from being alive on this beautiful earth.

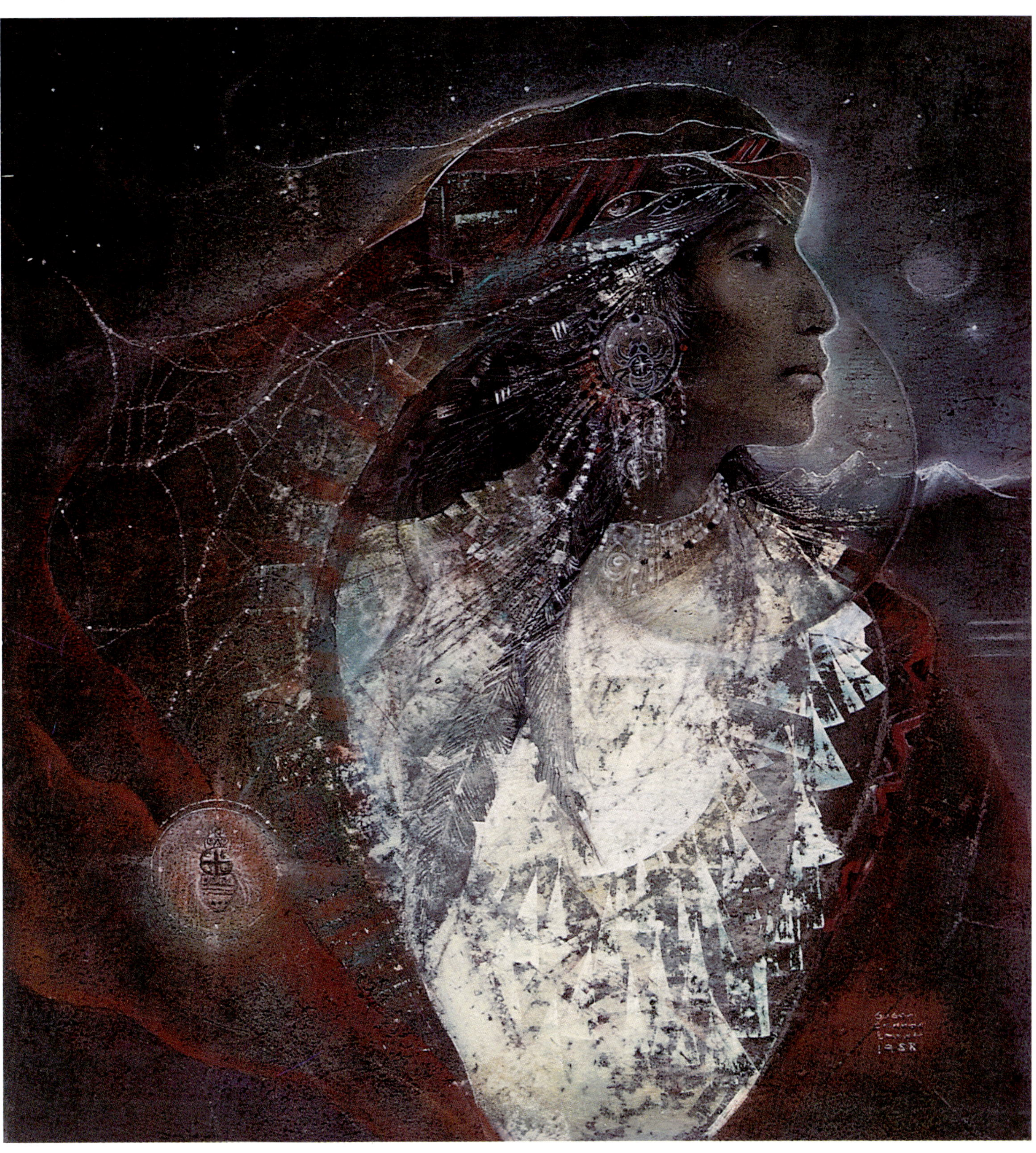